Chinese Made

Learning the Characters Through Illustrations

compiled by Cheng Chung Hing
translated and examined by Lin Wu Sun

Peace Book • Hai Feng Publishing Co.

© Hai Feng Publishing Co., 1999
ISBN 962-238-270-3
HF-288-P

Chinese Made – Learning the Characters Through Illustrations

Compiled by	Cheng Chung Hing
Translated and examined by	Lin Wu Sun
Illustrated by	Cao Wei Ye
Edited by	Irene Li

Published by   Hai Feng Publishing Co.
Rm.1502, Wing On House
71 Des Voeux Road, Central
Hong Kong

Printed by   Maison D'editions Quaille
Rm. 15, 8/F, Block A, Wah Tat Industrial Center
8-10 Wah Sing Street, Kwai Chung
Hong Kong

Format   190 x 206 mm
Edition   First Edition July 1999

Published & Printed in Hong Kong

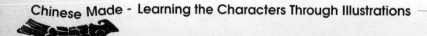

Preface

The American poet Ezra Pound once said, "The easiest language in the world for writing poetry is Chinese." And in the words of C. C. Cummings, another American poet, "Chinese poets are painters." This book, *Chinese made - Learning the Characters Through Illustrations*, is one which uses words to explain and pictures to illustrate the form and structure of Chinese characters. Therefore, it is both a collection of poetry and a picture album, so to speak.

In China, words and pictures have always been bound together. From very early times, people talked about writing and painting having the same origin. If you examine the Chinese character 書 (shū) and 畫 (huà) (in the complex version), you will find that they share the same upper radical (component part) which resembles a writing brush in the grip of a hand. Thus, 書 and 畫 both convey the idea of working with a brush. In this sense, they are verbs. On the other hand, they also represent the products of working with a brush, and in that sense, they are nouns.

書 畫 叢 中 尋 漢 字

It is not difficult to prove the relationship between the Chinese written character and poetry and painting. My friend, an overseas Chinese entrepreneur in Indonesia, Mr. Luo Haoran, or Ahmed Suriawinata, gave this example in his collection of prose *Watching the Clouds Gather*: "Consider the character 閒 which is quite interesting. It is a crescent moon seen through a crack between the two wings of a door." This may be a front door, a back door, or a window which opens in the middle. You push it open, raise your head and lift your eyes, and there in the sky is a clear, bright moon. You step out of the hall and immediately a pleasant, relaxed feeling fills your heart. To Mr. Luo, philology is a pastime only to be tended to after a day of battling in the business world, and yet his understanding of the Chinese character often surpasses that of a philologist. To him, the character 閒 not only presents a picture of the moon seen through the crack between the two panels of the door. It gives expression to an optimist's philosophy of life. I don't necessarily busy myself with what others are busy with; likewise, I may not feel at ease with something whereas others do. Only, when in the depth and quietude of night, one feels a peace and harmony within and without, only then can one be called a 閒人, "a man at ease." Mr. Luo's explanation is well-founded. Xu Kai of the Song Dynasty, in his *Shuo Wen Xi Zhuan*, an explanatory book on *Shuo Wen Jie Zi*, China's earliest study of Chinese written characters and their forms and origins, had this to say in reference to the character 閒: "The door is shut at night, yet one can still see the moon, for there's a slit in the door between the two wings."

Each Chinese character has a form of its own, representing a particular sound and a particular meaning, one at least. In other words, each character is a unity of form, sound and meaning. For every character, there is a form. There are as many "individuals" as there are characters. The student of Chinese must call on every one of the individuals if he or she is to really know the personality of each.

Learning Chinese is quite different from learning any other language. The

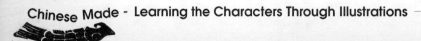

way of learning is different. In learning a Western language, for instance, you swallow a whole series of sounds, lock, stock and barrel. If you were to take a word apart, separating it into so many phonetic syllables, it would lose its meaning altogether. In learning Chinese, however, what you have to do is exactly that, not into so many syllables, but into so many characters. You learn first the characters, then the word. Take, for instance, the Chinese word 大學 (dà xué) which means "university". You first learn the words 大 and 學 separately since 大學 is formed by combining the two characters (you might call them elements of language). In meaning, 大學 has to do with both 大 and 學, and yet 大學 is not a simple case of 大 plus 學. It does not mean a big school (大的學校), nor a school for adults (大人的學校), and certainly not what was called (大家來學), everyone a student, a slogan in vogue during the decade of the so-called "Cultural Revolution." 大學 is the Chinese equivalent of the English word "university." But if you were to take the English word "university" and try to figure out its meaning based on the meanings of the five syllabic components u/ni/ver/si/ty, you would definitely get nowhere, because separately, these components have no meaning at all and certainly have nothing to do with what the word "university" means. So, the character forms the basis in learning Chinese, whereas the word or sentence forms the basis for learning a Western language. It is no wonder then that there should have been so many textbooks written since ancient times on learning Chinese characters, e.g. *Qian Zi Wen* (Learn A Thousand Characters) and *Bai Jia Xin* (One Hundred Family Names).

In Chinese, the character is the unit carrier of meaning whereas in English, it is the word that serves the same purpose. Each language in the world has its unique features, the same is true with the written script. One is always, consciously or unconsciously, interpreting another language and its written script on the basis of the characteristics of the language he or she first came into contact with in life. With respect to the Chinese language, one needs to study and appreciate its characters one by one, picture by picture, as one would in analysing and appreciating a work of art.

The pictures as represented in the Chinese characters vary in complexity. Take the characters contained in this book. Some are as simple as 人, 口, 牛, 羊; others as complicated as 雙, 養, 喜, 聲 Whether simple or complicated, they are each a picture and a poem. Of course, one cannot expect everyone to agree in their analyses of each and every character, just as people couldn't totally agree, in fact they might totally disagree, in their understanding and interpretation of a painting or a poem. Once a painting or a poem has been made public, the copyright, materially speaking, belongs to the work's creator; spiritually, however, it belongs to the whole society. Regardless of whether the poet or painter agrees or disagrees, the reader or viewer would have his own appreciation of the work on the basis of his or her own understanding. The same holds true, more or less, for the written script. It is your right to create the written character, it is my right to interpret it. Take the case of 章(zhāng). Its original meaning was "the end", "conclusion", or "a temporary close of something." The book *Shuo Wen* says, "When the music finishes, it's a 章, which is made up of 音 (yīn, meaning music) and 十(shī, meaning ten), for 十 is the limit of numbers." Chinese think of 十 as to mean "many", "complete"or "perfect." Hence the idiom 十全十美, meaning "perfect in every way", and the idiom of the drinkers wager 十滿大堂, meaning "ten, the largest of all." When a melody reaches its end, one might say "the music has reached 十 (ten)." So, to say that the character 章 is the combination of 音 and 十 seems more like the original intent of the word's creator. And yet, 99% of the people consider 章 to be the combination of 立 and 早. In both the *Comprehensive Dictionary of Chinese Characters* and the *Comprehensive Dictionary of Chinese Words*, two authoritative dictionaries of the day, 章 is listed in the section under the radical 立 and not the section under the radical 音 or 十. Even people surnamed 章, when introducing themselves, choose to define their surname as 章, 立 plus 早.

There is yet another well-known example, the character 東. This was originally written as 橐. Inscribed on oracle bones, it resembled a bag tied up at both ends. Later, an explanatory note in *Shuo Wen* put it as "the sun half way up

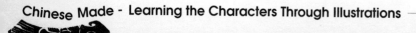

Chinese Made - Learning the Characters Through Illustrations

the tree," indicating that the sun has newly risen over the horizon and has not yet reached the top of the tree. When the sun reaches a height above the top of the tree, it is represented by the character 杲, and when it has sunk to below the bottom of the tree, it is represented by the character 杳. Thus, the three characters 橐,杲,杳 form a series illustrating the cycle from sunrise to sunset. *Shuo Wen's* explanation of the character 橐 therefore, seems quite acceptable. We might call the early explanations orthodox, and the later ones, common. Orthodox or common, they both serve to depict the origin of the Chinese character. We certainly shouldn't criticise those who describe 章 as a combination of 立 and 早, or the one who said that 橐 indicates "the sun is half way up the tree". Nevertheless, there has to be a limit to how common you can get. For instance, we must not imitate the fortune teller who does his job by taking apart and analysing the component parts of a character. That is not science. In this respect, this book *Chinese Made - Learning the Characters Through Illustrations* has achieved a good balance between the orthodox and the common. In present-day terms, this little book is both interesting and scientific.

For some time now, a theory has been going around among linguistic circles to the effect that all written languages in the world have to go through a process of elevation from being pictographic to ideographic to phonetic. According to this theory, the phonetic written language is the most developed of the three because it no longer has any link with meaning but only with sound. Thus, with only a small number of letters, one can spell out all the words there are. Judging by this standard, the Chinese character which remains at the ideographic stage is naturally not up to the standard of a developed language. A great man therefore pointed out that "The Chinese character must be reformed. It must follow the common orientation of the world's languages, that is the use of phonetic alphabet to replace the characters." However, it seems that the pictographic feature of the Chinese character cannot be changed overnight. Moreover, in this era, as the computer step by step enters every organisation, every office room, every school and even every home, the unique pictographic

feature of the Chinese character is more and more demonstrating its superiority. Thousands upon thousands of Chinese character-pictures have made their way to the computer terminal at a speed which equals, if not surpasses, that of the phonetic languages. They not only record the history of the Chinese civilization but serves the present-day purpose of uniting the Chinese nation and maintaining the country's unification. The Chinese written character and the Chinese nation share a common fate. If you wish to learn about this nation and its history and culture, you would find it hard to fulfil that wish without learning the characters.

Chinese Made - *Learning the Characters Through Illustration* is written for those non-Chinese who intend to explore the secrets of the Chinese civilization. It is somewhat like a guidebook, listing more than a hundred cultural sites. Like the looking glass in *Alice in Wonderland*, the characters depicted in this book will take the tourist into the kaleidoscopic world that is Chinese culture. For people who are just beginning to have any contact with China, imagine yourself still inside a room, but with the help of this book, you will see "through the crack in the door" the clear, bright moon outside, or even the stars twinkling in the sky.

by Cheng Xianghui,
Dean of College of Chinese Language,
University of Macao, June 4, 1998

Contents

Chinese Made - Learning the Characters Through Illustrations

書畫叢中尋漢字

ài
(mountain pass)

隘

A pictogram. " 阝 " on the left is an abbreviation of 阜, meaning a tall mountain. The other half, 益, meaning addition, implies that an earthen defence is built on the top of a mountain. The combination means a place which is strategically located and difficult of access, or simply a mountain pass.

隘口	àikǒu	(mountain) pass
隘路	àilù	narrow passage
隘巷	àixiàng	a narrow lane; alley
要隘	yào'ài	a strategic pass
狭隘	xiá'ài	narrow-minded

心胸狹隘
xīn xiōng xiá ài
narrow-minded; intolerant
狹隘的山道
xiá ài de shān dào
mountain trail

Example:

到那個村莊的最短路線不是途經那條主公路，而是一條狹窄的、簇葉叢生的隘路。

Dào nàge cūnzhuāng de zuì duǎn lùxiàn búshì tú jīng nà tiáo zhǔgōnglù, érshì yì tiáo xiázhǎi de, cùyè cóngshēng de àilù.

The shortest route to the village isn't by the main road but by a narrow, overgrown track.

àn

(dark; hidden)

暗

This pictophonetic character comprises two parts. On the left is the character 日 (sun), and on the right 音 (hidden, secret). The combination suggests darkness due to insufficient light.

暗藏	àncáng	hide; conceal
暗娼	ànchāng	unlicensed (or unregistered) prostitute
暗淡	àndàn	dim; faint
暗害	ànhài	kill secretly; stab in the back
暗井	ànjǐng	blind shaft; winze
暗探	àntàn	secret agent; detective
暗笑	ànxiào	laugh in (or up) one's sleeve; snigger
暗語	ànyǔ	code word

Chinese Made - *Learning the Characters Through Illustrations*

暗無天日
àn wú tiān rì
complete darkness; total absence of justice
暗渡陳倉
àn dù chén cāng
do one thing under the cover of another; illicit activities
暗送秋波
àn sòng qiū bō
make eyes at sb. while others are not looking; make secret overtures to sb.

暗 暗 暊

Example:

他暗示要我走開。
Tā ànshì yào wǒ zǒu kāi.
He hinted that he wanted me to leave.

15

bǎi

(a hundred)

百

By comparing two ancient Chinese pictograms " ◊ " and " ◊ ", both pronounced as *bai*, we find the latter is derived from the former, which means white or bright. How it came to mean a hundred is not clear.

百般	bǎibān	in a hundred and one ways; in every possible way; by every means
百倍	bǎibèi	a hundredfold; a hundred times
百部	bǎibù	the tuber of stemona (*Stemona japonica* or *Stemona sessilifolia*)
百貨	bǎihuò	general merchandise
百年	bǎinián	a hundred years; a century
百萬	bǎiwàn	million
百姓	bǎixìng	common people
百合	bǎihé	lily

百讀不懨
bǎi dú bú yàn
be worth reading a hundred times

百感交集
bǎi gǎn jiāo jí
all sorts of fellings well up in one's heart

百孔千瘡
bǎi kǒng qiān chuāng
riddled with gaping wounds; afflicted with all ills

百川歸海
bǎi chuān guī hǎi
all rivers flow to the sea; all things tend in one direction

百思不解
bǎi sī bù jiě
remain puzzled after pondering over sth. a hundred times; remain perplexed despite much thought

百尺竿頭，更進一步
bǎi chǐ gān tóu, gèng jìn yí bù
make still further progress

Example:

這個故事百聽不懨。
Zhèige gùshi bǎi tīng bú yàn.
You never get tired of hearing this story.

書 畫 叢 中 尋 漢 字

běi
(north)

北

An ideogram. This character was originally written as 背. It derived from "从" found on oracle bones depicting two persons sitting with their backs to each other. Ancient Chinese used to think that facing the south was the correct way of sitting, while facing the north was thought to be sitting backward. Hence the old saying, "his Majesty sits facing the south while his ministers pay their respects facing the north."

北斗星	běidǒuxīng	the Big Dipper; the Plough
北方	běifāng	north; the northern part of the country, esp. the area north of the Huanghe River; the North
北極	běijí	the North Pole; the Arctic Pole; the north magnetic pole
北京	Běijīng	Beijing (Peking)
北美洲	Běiměizhōu	North America
北溫帶	běiwēndài	the north temperate zone
敗北	bàiběi	defeat

Chinese Made - Learning the Characters Through Illustrations

北伐戰爭
Běifá Zhànzhēng
the Northern Expedition (1926-1927)

北國風光
běi guó fēng guāng
northern scenery

北回歸線
běi huí guī xiàn
the Tropic of Cancer

北洋軍閥
Běi Yáng Jūnfá
the Northern Warlords (1912-1927)

Example:

我生在南方，但從小生活在北方。
Wǒ shēng zài nánfāng, dàn cóng xiǎo shēnghuó zài běifāng.
I was born in the South, but I've settled in the North since my childhood.

bèi

(cowrie; shellfish)

貝

A pictogram, "貝" refers to the empty shell which remains after the meat of the clam inside is removed. Its origin found on oracle bones looked like this "🐚". The upper part "🐚" represents the shell and the lower part "∕ ∖" the clam's two feelers. From the artifacts unearthed by archaeologists, we discover that the primitive people were very fond of decorating themselves with stringed shells.

貝雕	bèidiāo	shell carving
貝殼	bèiké	shell
貝類	bèilèi	shellfish; molluscs
貝母	bèimǔ	the bulb of fritillary (*Fritillaria thunbergii*)
貝丘	bèiqiū	shell mound

貝殼細工
bèi ké xì gōng
shell work
貝闕珠宮
bèi què zhū gōng
underwater palace decorated with shells and pearls; imperial palace

Example:

孩子們在海中拾到許多貝殼。

Háizi men zài hǎizhōng shí dào xǔduō bèiké.

The children picked up many sea shells at the seashore.

bēn

(to run)

奔

Ideogram. In metal language *"夲", the upper part "大" shows a man running with swaying arms and the lower part "芔", three feet, depicting the rapid movement of his legs. A clear sign that a man is running. The present form of the character was evolved from the *Little Zhuan* (script used during Qin Dynasty, 221-206 BC, and which appeared later than metal language). It is thus indistinguishable from its original form.

*scripts inscribed on bronzes found prior to Qin Dynasty.

奔波	bēnbō	rush about; be busy running about
奔馳	bēnchí	run quickly; speed
奔跑	bēnpǎo	run
奔襲	bēnxí	long-range raid
奔瀉	bēnxiè	(of torrents) rush down; pour down
奔走	bēnzǒu	run; rush about; be busy running about

奔走呼號
bēn zǒu hū hào
go around campaigning for a cause

熱情奔放
rè qíng bēn fàng
overflowing with enthusiasm

四散奔逃
sì sàn bēn táo
flee in all directions; flee helter-skelter; stampede

鐵水奔流
tiě shuǐ bēn liú
molten iron pouring out in a stream; racing current

長江之水，奔騰不息
Chángjiāng zhī shuǐ, bēn téng bù xī
The mighty waters of the Changjiang roll on incessantly.

奔走相告
bēn zǒu xiāng gào
run around spreading the news; lose no time in telling each other the news

Example:

駿馬在草原上奔馳。
Jùnmǎ zài cǎoyuán shang bēnchí.
Sturdy steeds gallop on the grasslands.

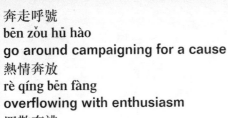

23

bí

(nose)

鼻

The original form of this character was 自, which has the shape of a nose. Pronounced as *zi*, it was later extended to mean self. When 畀 (pronounced as *bi*) is placed below 自, it is pronounced as *bi*, meaning the nose. 畀 means to give. In breathing, one has to inhale and exhale, which is a form of give-and-take.

鼻竇	bídòu	paranasal sinus
鼻孔	bíkǒng	nostril
鼻腔	bíqiāng	nasal cavity
鼻塞	bísāi	have a stuffy nose
鼻淵	bíyuān	nasosinusitis
鼻祖	bízǔ	the earliest ancestor; originator (of a tradition, school of thought, etc.)
鼻煙壺	bíyānhú	snuff bottle

鼻青臉腫
bí qīng liǎn zhǒng
a bloody nose and a swollen face

電光鼻鏡
diàn guǎng bí jìng
nasoscope

鷹鉤鼻子
yīng gōu bí zi
aquiline nose; Roman nose

Example:

不要只顧鼻子底下的小事。
Búyào zhǐ gù bízi dǐ xià de xiǎoshì.
Don't get bogged down in trivial matters.

書畫叢中尋漢字

biǎo
(surface; outside)
表

An ideogram composed of 衣 (clothes) and 毛 (hair). Written as "𧘇" in *Little Zhuan*, the upper part is represents hair or fur and the lower part, clothes. The ancients used to wear animal fur to protect themselves against the cold. When they did so, the hairy side was always put on the outside. However, unless one is told, one can hardly discern the 毛 "𡕽" part of this character.

表白	biǎobái	vindicate
表層	biǎocéng	surface layer
表達	biǎodá	express; convey
表觀	biǎoguān	apparent
表決	biǎojué	decide by vote
表露	biǎolù	show; reveal
表面	biǎomiàn	surface; outside appearance
表情	biǎoqíng	express one's fellings
表態	biǎotài	make known one's position, declare where one stands

Chinese Made - Learning the Characters Through Illustrations

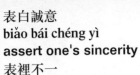

表白誠意
biǎo bái chéng yì
assert one's sincerity

表裡不一
biǎo lǐ bù yī
think in one way and behave in another

表面現象
biǎo miàn xiàn xiàng
superficial phenomenon

表明立場
biǎo míng lì chǎng
make known one's position

表現手法
biǎo xiàn shǒu fǎ
technique of expression

表意文字
biǎo yì wén zì
ideograph

Example:

我激動的心情難以用語言來表達。
Wǒ jīdòng de xīnqíng nán yǐ yòng yǔyán lái biǎodá.
Words can hardly express my excitement.

cǎi

(to pick)

采

An ideogram. In metal language "ᗭ", it comprised of the hand "⺥" and tree "朩" characters. By association, it indicates picking fruits or leaves on the tree.

採伐	cǎifá	fell; cut
採訪	cǎifǎng	gather material
採購	cǎigòu	make purchases for an organization or enterprise
採集	cǎijí	gather; collect
採礦	cǎikuàng	mining
採用	cǎiyòng	adopt; use; employ
採擇	cǎizé	select and adopt
採摘	cǎizhāi	pick

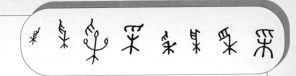

採伐跡地
cǎi fá jì dì
cutover

採錄民歌
cǎi lù mín gē
collect and record folk songs

採取攻勢
cǎi qǔ gōng shì
take the offensive

地下採礦
dì xià cǎi kuàng
underground mining

蒸汽採暖
zhēng qì cǎi nuǎn
steam heating

Example:

我們今天早晨去採集昆蟲標本好嗎？
Wǒmén jīntiān zǎochén qù cǎijí kūnchóng biāoběn hǎo ma?
Shall we go collecting insect specimen this morning?

cè

(volume; book)

Pictogram. We know that before the invention of paper-making, ancient Chinese used to write on wooden or bamboo strips. The length and width of these strips were standardised so that they could be tied together by a piece of string or ox-hide band. When this was done, a volume "册" was ready for use.

册頁	cèyè	an album of paintings or calligraphy
册子	cèzi	book; volume
名册	míngcè	namelist
畫册	huàcè	picture album
紀念册	jìniàncè	album

裝訂成冊
zhuāng dìng chéng cè
bind into book form

載入史冊
zǎi rù shǐ cè
go down in history

Example:

這本書已銷售十萬冊。
Zhèi běn shū yǐ xiāoshòu shíwàn cè.
100,000 copies of the book have been sold.

書畫叢中尋漢字

cháo

(nest)

巢

Pictogram. In *Little Zhuan*, the character was written as " 巢 ", the top part "巛" representing three birds, the middle part "臼" a nest, and the lower part "木" a tree. As you might have guessed, the character means a bird nest on a tree.

巢菜	cháocài	common vetch
巢蛾	cháo'é	ermine moth
巢鼠	cháoshǔ	harvest mouse
巢穴	cháoxuè	lair; den; nest; hideout
匪巢	fěicháo	nest (or den) of robbers; bandits' lair
鳥巢	niǎocháo	bird's nest

雀巢咖啡
què cháo kā fēi
Nescafe

直搗巢穴
zhǐ dǎo cháo xuè
attack the enemy's lair; destroy the bandits' den

蜜蜂蜂巢
mì fēng fēng cháo
honeycomb

共築愛巢
gòng zhù ài cháo
set up their own love nest

Example:

再壞的鳥也不會弄髒自己的窩巢。
Zài huài de niǎo yě búhuì nòngzāng zìjǐ de wōcháo.
It is an ill bird that fouls his own nest.

書畫叢中尋漢字

chē

(chariot; car; vehicle)

車

Pictogram. In metal language, it looked like a bird's-eye view of a vehicle " ". The horizontal line " " at the bottom represents the axle, " " the carriage, the two vertical lines " " on its left and right the two wheels, and " " in front, shafts for the two horses or oxen. In ancient times, 車 generally meant two-wheeled chariots.

車道	chēdào	(traffic) lane
車隊	chēduì	motorcade
車禍	chēhuò	traffic (or road) accident
車輪	chēlún	wheel (of a vehicle)
車票	chēpiào	train or bus ticket; ticket
車站	chēzhàn	station; depot; stop

車水馬龍
chē shuǐ mǎ lóng
heavy traffic

車載斗量
chē zǎi dǒu liáng
enough to fill carts and be measured by the *dou*

i.e., common and numerous

沉割車刀
chén gē chē dāo
under-cutting turning tool

來往車輛
lái wǎng chē liàng
traffic

裝配車間
zhuāng pèi chē jiān
assembly shop

車到山前必有路
chē dào shān qián bì yǒu lù
The cart will find its way round the hill when it gets there.

i.e., Things will eventually sort themselves out.

Example:

在我們這裡像我這樣的人車載斗量，不可勝數。
Zài wǒmen zhèlǐ xiàng wǒ zhèyàng de rén chē zǎi dǒu liáng, bù kě shèng shǔ.
Where I come from, people like me come by the bushel.

chuān

(river; waterway)

川

Pictogram. On oracle bones, it was " 𝕝 ", which indicates water flowing between river banks. In metal language, it evolved to three curved lines " 𝕝 ", giving a better presentation to the way water flows in a river.

川貝	chuānbèi	tendril-leaved fritillary bulb
川劇	chuānjù	Sichuan opera
川芎	chuānxiōng	the rhizome of Chuanxiong (*Ligusticum wallichii*)
川資	chuānzī	travelling expenses

高山大川
gāo shān dà chuān
high mountains and big rivers
一馬平川
yì mǎ píng chuān
a vast expanse of flat land; a great stretch of land
川流不息
chuān liú bù xī
flowing past in an endless stream

Example:

在大川大海中鍛鍊自己。
Zài dàchuān dàhǎi zhōng duànliàn zìjǐ.
Temper oneself in big rivers and seas.

書畫叢中尋漢字

dà

(big; great)

大

Pictogram. From oracle bones, we can see that "大" looked like the frontal view of a man who is stretching his arms and legs to the limit in order to demonstrate his breadth. The character therefore means great and broad.

大敗	dàbài	defeat utterly; put to rout
大腸	dàcháng	large intestine
大潮	dàcháo	spring tide
大膽	dàdǎn	bold; daring
大刀	dàdāo	broadsword
大方	dàfang	generous; liberal; easy
大樓	dàlóu	multi-storied building

Chinese Made - Learning the Characters Through Illustrations

大筆一揮
dà bǐ yì huī
with one stroke of the pen

大慈大悲
dà cí dà bēi
infinitely merciful

大發雷霆
dà fā léi tíng
be furious; fly into a rage; bawl at sb. angrily

大功告成
dà gōng gào chéng
(of a project, work, etc.) be accomplished; be crowned with success

大惑不解
dà huò bù jiě
be extremely puzzled; be unable to make head or tail of sth.

大千世界
dà qiān shì jiè
the boundless universe

大失所望
dà shī suǒ wàng
greatly disappointed; to one's great disappointment

大義滅親
dà yì miè qīn
place righteousness above family loyalty

大事化小，小事化了
dà shì huà xiǎo, xiǎo shì huà liǎo
down play a problem or ignore it altogether

Example:

這種料子的顏色和花樣很大方。
Zhèizhǒng liàozi de yánsè hé huāyàng hěn dàfang.
The pattern and colour of this fabric are in good taste.

書畫叢中尋漢字

dàn

(sunrise)

且

Ideogram. It was written like this " ☉ " on oracle bones. The top part " ⊖ " represent the sun, and the symbol below " ◘ " the earth. When the sun emerges from the earth, it is of course sunrise.

一旦	yídàn	in a single day; once; in case
元旦	yuándàn	New Year's Day
旦暮	dànmù	day and night; in a short period of time
旦夕	dànxi	morning and evening; in a short while
旦角	dànjiǎo	female role in Peking Opera

旦夕之間
dàn xī zhī jiān
in a day's time; overnight
危在旦夕
wēi zài dàn xī
in imminent danger
旦不保夕
dàn bù bǎo xī
face instant danger; in a precarious situation
旦暮入地
dàn mù rù dì
with one leg in the grave
通宵達旦
tōng xiāo dá dàn
all night long; all through the night

Example:

他們相處多年，一旦分別，不免依依不捨。
Tāmen xiāngchù duōnián, yídàn fēnbié bùmiǎn yīyī bùshě.
After being together for years, they can't bear to part from each other.

書畫叢中尋漢字

dǎo

(island)

島

Pictophonetic character. Formed by combining the characters bird (鳥) and mountain (山). The ancients considered that which emerged from the surface of the sea a mountain. By merging the chirping of the birds with the sound of splashing waves, the character 島 is created.

島國	dǎoguó	country consisting of one or more islands; island country
島嶼	dǎoyǔ	islands and islets; islands
孤島	gūdǎo	desert island
小島	xiǎodǎo	small island
安全島	ānquándǎo	safety island; pedestrian island

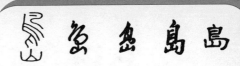

島上居民
dǎo shàng jū mín
islander
越島作戰
yuè dǎo zuò zhàn
island hopping

Example:

他受困於荒島之上。
Tā shòukùn yú huāngdǎo zhī shàng.
He was marooned on a desert island.

dé
(virtue)

德

An ideogram. That which is straight-forward and comes from the heart is virtuous (德), i.e., say what you feel and do what you think is right. In this character, the 直 (meaning straight) component is turned sideways "罒" while retaining the horizontal line below, which makes it look like this "罒". So from now on, please don't forget the horizontal line when you write the character 德.

德國	Déguó	Germany
德行	déxíng	moral conduct
德語	déyǔ	German (language)
德育	déyù	moral education
德政	dézhèng	benevolent rule
德治	dézhì	rule of virtue

同心同德
tóng xīn tóng dé
be of one heart and one mind

德才兼備
dé cái jiān bèi
have both ability and political integrity

德高望重
dé gāo wàng zhòng
be of noble character and hight prestige; enjoy high prestige and command universal respect

以怨報德
yǐ yuàn bào dé
return evil for good; repay kindness with ingratitude; bite the hand that feeds you

Example:

那個傢伙真德行。
Nàge jiāhuo zhěn déxing.
That fellow is really disgusting.

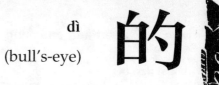

dì
(bull's-eye)

的

Pictogram, composed of 白(white) and 勺. In archery, the white spot in the centre of the target is the bull's-eye and 勺 indicates the circle around it. Notice it has a dot in the centre. When the archer's arrow hits the bull's-eye, he is said to have 中的. Usually, in an archery context, you have your eye " 目 " fixed on the bull's-eye, that is how the expression 目的 (purpose) came into use.

目的	mùdì	purpose; aim; goal; objective
目的地	mùdìdì	destination
的確	díquè	indeed; really

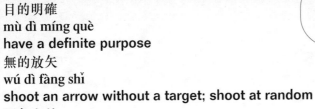

目的明確
mù dì míng què
have a definite purpose

無的放矢
wú dì fàng shǐ
shoot an arrow without a target; shoot at random

眾矢之的
zhòng shǐ zhī dì
target of public criticism (or censure)

Example:

他們安全抵達了目的地。
Tāmen ānquán dǐdá le mùdìdì.
They arrived at the destination safely.

書畫叢中尋漢字

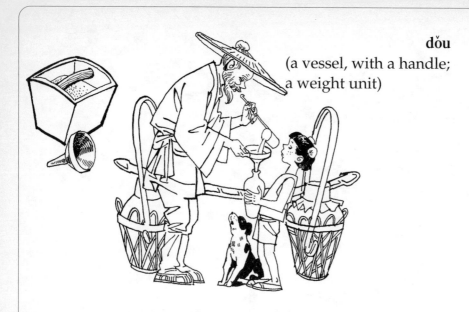

dǒu
(a vessel, with a handle;
a weight unit)

斗

Pictogram. In metal language, it was written as "ᘐ", the top part "⊃" showing a vessel and the lower part "丅" its handle. That is exactly what it means. By implication, it becomes a weight unit.

斗膽	dǒudǎn	make bold
斗拱	dǒugǒng	*dougong*, a system of brackets inserted between the top of column and a crossbeam (each bracket being formed of a double bow-shaped arm, called *gong*, which supports a block of wood, called *dou*, in each side)
斗笠	dǒulì	bamboo hat
斗篷	dǒupeng	cape; cloak
斗渠	dǒuqú	lateral canal
斗室	dǒushì	a samll room
漏斗	lòudǒu	funnel
煙斗	yāndǒu	(tobacco) pipe

斗米尺布
dǒu mǐ chǐ bù
little food and cloth
斗轉星移
dǒu zhuǎn xīng yí
the day dawns
斗酒隻雞
dǒu jiǔ zhī jī
simple meal; to commemorate the death of a dear one with wine and chicken
車載斗量
chē zǎi dǒu liáng
enough to fill carts and be measured by the *dou*

i.e., common and numerous

Example:

我斗膽説一句，這件事您做錯了。
Wǒ dǒudǎn shuō yí jù, zhèi jiàn shì nín zuò cuò le.
May I make bold to suggest that you were wrong to do so.

書畫叢中尋漢字

dòu

(tussle; fight)

Pictogram. From the symbol "" on oracle bones, we can distinguish two men engaged in a fight, their arms () locked in a tussle. Hence fighting against each other. By extension, it also means a contest.

鬥雞	dòujī	gamecock; cockfighting
鬥氣	dòuqì	quarrel or contend with sb. on account of a personal grudge
鬥眼	dòuyǎn	cross-eye
鬥爭	dòuzhēng	struggle; fight; combat
鬥志	dòuzhì	will to fight
鬥智	dòuzhì	battle of wits

鬥智昂揚
dòu zhì áng yáng
have high morale
鼓舞鬥志
gǔ wǔ dòu zhì
arouse the fighting will
鬥雞走狗
dòu jī zǒu gǒu
cock fight and dog race, an ancient form of Chinese gambling somewhat like horse-racing

Example:

雖然屢遭敗績，他們仍甚有鬥志。
Suīrán lǚ zāo bàijì, tāmen réng shèn yǒu dòuzhì.
In spite of numerous defeates, they still had plenty of fight left in them.

書畫叢中尋漢字

ér

(child; son)

兒

Pictograph. In oracle bones "ㄓ", the lower part is a person "ㄱ" and the upper part a human head "ㄩ", with the fontanel not yet fully developed. This indicates he is still a child.

兒歌	érgē	children's song; nursery rhymes
兒科	érkē	(department of) paediatrics
兒女	érnǚ	sons and daughters
兒孫	érsūn	children and grandchildren; descendants; posterity
兒童	értóng	children
兒媳	érxí	daughter-in-law
兒戲	érxì	trifling matter
兒子	érzi	son

Chinese Made - Learning the Characters Through Illustrations

兒科醫生
ér kē yī shēng
paediatrician

兒女情長
ér nǚ qíng cháng
be immersed in love

兒童讀物
ér tóng dú wù
children's books

兒童醫院
ér tóng yī yuàn
children's hospital

英雄兒女
yīng xíong ér nǚ
young heroes and heroines

Example:

他有一兒一女。
Tā yǒu yì ér yì nǚ.
He has a son and a daughter.

fàn
(criminal)

犯

"犭" (犭) on the left is the symbol for a dog; "已" on the right originally looked like "已", which represents a person seated. The meaning of this character is derived from the situation when a criminal is tired from standing a long time, he is allowed to sit down, but a dog is called in to keep watch on him.

犯案	fàn'àn	be found out and brought to justice
犯病	fànbìng	have an attack of one's old illness
犯愁	fànchóu	worry; be anxious
犯法	fànfǎ	violate (or break) the law
犯規	fànguī	break the rules
犯忌	fànjì	violate a taboo
犯人	fànrén	prisoner
犯罪	fànzuì	commit a crime (or an offence)
犯不着	fànbuzháo	not worthwhile

犯法行為
fàn fǎ xíng wéi
offence against the law
犯罪分子
fàn zuì fèn zǐ
offender; criminal
犯罪行為
fàn zuì xíng wéi
criminal offence
侵人犯規
qīn rén fàn guī
personal foul

犭 犯 犯 犯 犯

Example:

他的氣喘病又犯了。
Tā de qìchuǎn bìng yòu fàn le.
He's got another attack of asthma.

fēi
(imperial concubine;
princess)

妃

This ideogram has two parts. The left being a woman (女) and the right self (己).
Originally, 妃 meant a man's wife, implying that "the woman is mine". Later it
became a special term for the emperor's concubines who ranked next to the
queen.

妃嬪	fēipín	imperial concubines of all ranks
妃色	fēisè	light pink
妃子	fēizi	imperial concubine
貴妃	guìfēi	imperial concubine of the highest rank
王妃	wángfēi	princess

Chinese Made - *Learning the Characters Through Illustrations*

貴妃醉酒
guì fēi zuì jiǔ
The Drunken Beauty, a Peking Opera about
an emperor and his favourite concubine

Example:

在古代，中國皇帝有三宮六院七十二妃。

Zài gǔdài, Zhōngguó huángdì yǒu sān gōng liù yuàn qī shí èr fēi.

In ancient times, Chinese emperors had three empresses, six high-ranking imperial concubines and seventy-two ordinary concubines.

書畫叢中尋漢字

fēi

(wrong; no)

非

Pictogram. This character was originally a homophone and synonym of the character 飛. From metal language "兆", we can detect a bird flapping its wings. However, as the Chinese language developed, this character lost its original meaning and came to mean "wrong" in the expression 是非 (right and wrong), and unusually or abnormal in the expression 非常.

非常	fēicháng	extraordinary; unusual; special
非但	fēidàn	not only
非法	fēifǎ	illegal; unlawful; illicit
非凡	fēifán	outstanding; extraordinary; uncommon
非分	fēifèn	overstepping one's bounds; assuming
非命	fēimìng	die a violent death
非難	fēinàn	blame; censure, reproach
非議	fēiyì	reproach; censure

非比尋常
fēi bǐ xún cháng
unusual

非親非故
fēi qīn fēi gù
neither relative nor friend; neither kith nor kin

非此即彼
fēi cǐ jí bǐ
either this or that; one or the other

非公莫入
fēi gōng mò rù
no admittance except on business

非同小可
fēi tóng xiǎo kě
no small (or trivial) matter

分清是非
fēn qīng shì fēi
distinguish between right and wrong

為非作歹
wéi fēi zuò dǎi
do evil

Example:

他非但自己幹得好，還肯幫助別人。
Tā fēidàn zìjǐ gàn de hǎo, hái kěn bāngzhù biérén.
He not only does his own work well, but is also ready to help others.

書畫叢中尋漢字

fèn
(lift oneself;
exert oneself)

奮

Pictogram. In its original form, this character was written as "奮". The lower part "⊕" represents the land, or the ground. The upper part "奮" is a bird with its wings flapping. A bird in rapid ascent needs to make an effort, therefore this character means to lift oneself and by extension, act vigorously.

奮鬥	fèndòu	struggle; fight; strive
奮發	fènfā	rouse oneself; exert oneself
奮力	fènlì	do all one can
奮勉	fènmiǎn	make a determined effort
奮起	fènqǐ	rise with force and spirit
奮勇	fènyǒng	summon up all one's courage and energy
奮戰	fènzhàn	fight bravely

奮起直追
fèn qǐ zhí zhui
do all one can to catch up

奮鬥到底
fèn dòu dào dǐ
fight to the bitter end

奮不顧身
fèn bú gù shēn
dash ahead regardless of one's safety

奮發圖強
fèn fā tú qiáng
go all out to make the country strong; work hard for the prosperity of the country

Example:

騎兵戰士衝入敵群，奮力砍殺。
Qíbing zhànshi chōngrù díqún, fènlì kǎnshā.
The cavalrymen charged into the enemy ranks, slashing furiously.

書畫叢中尋漢字

fú

(good furtune;
happiness; blessing)

Pictophonetic character. In ancient times, the character was written as "祇". The "☖" on the right depicts a wine flask while "示" on the left represents offering to the ancestors or heaven. When the ancients made offerings, they sprinkled wine on the ground, believing this would bring good luck to themselves.

福分	fúfen	good fortune
福利	fúlì	material benefits; well-being; welfare
福氣	fúqi	happy lot; good furtune
福星	fúxing	lucky star; mascot
福音	fúyin	Gospel; glad tidings

福利設施
fú lì shè shī
welfare facilities

福利事業
fú lì shì yè
welfare projects (or services)

造福人類
zào fú rén lèi
promote the well-being of mankind

Example:

你可不能身在福中不知福啊！
Nǐ kě bùnéng shēn zài fú zhōng bù zhī fú a!
Don't take your good fortune for granted.

gāo

(lamb; kid)

羔

An ideogram. We can almost guess what it means just by looking at its original form "羔". The upper part "羊" symbolises a sheep and the lower part "火" a fire, indicating the roasting of mutton. The ancient Chinese already knew that barbecued mutton was especially delicious. Later on 羔 came to mean simply lamb.

羔皮	gāopí	lambskin; kidskin; kid
羔羊	gāoyáng	lamb; kid
羔子	gāozi	lamb; kid; fawn

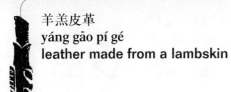

羊羔皮革
yáng gāo pí gé
leather made from a lambskin

Example:

房屋後有一些羊羔。
Fángwū hòu yǒu yìxiē yánggāo.
There are some lambs behind the house.

gōng

(fair; just)

Pictogram. In metal language, it was written as " ᗜ ". The lower part " ▽ " represents an open jar while ")(" on the top represents even distribution of the stuff inside. Hence the meaning: fair or just.

公案	gōng'àn	a complicated legal case
公佈	gōngbù	promulgate; announce; publish; make public
公道	gōngdao	fair; just; reasonable; impartial
公德	gōngdé	social morality; social ethics
公開	gōngkāi	open, overt; public
公理	gōnglǐ	generally acknowledged truth; self-evident truth
公眾	gōngzhòng	the public
公敵	gōngdí	public enemy

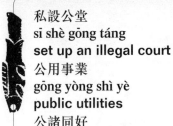

私設公堂
sī shè gōng táng
set up an illegal court

公用事業
gōng yòng shì yè
public utilities

公諸同好
gōng zhū tóng hào
share enjoyment with those of the same taste

公之於世
gōng zhī yú shì
make known to the world; reveal to the public

買賣公平
mǎi mài gōng píng
be fair in buying and selling; buy and sell at reasonable prices

公報私仇
gōng bào sī chóu
avenge a personal wrong in the name of public interest; abuse public power to retaliate on personal enemy

Example:

我還有很多公事要辦。
Wǒ hái yǒu hěnduō gōngshì yào bàn.
I still have a lot of official duties to attend to.

guǎ

(alone; few)

寡

Ideogram consisting of two parts. The top "宀" represents a house or a room, underneath it is 頌. Split into two parts, one placed on top of the other to form "寡". The accent here is separation. Just as the two parts are separated, when a person is separated from his peers and kept in a house all by himself, he is alone.

寡婦	guǎfù	widow
寡人	guǎrén	I, the sovereign; we
寡頭	guǎtóu	oligarch
守寡	shóuguǎ	live in widowhood
鰥寡	guānguǎ	widowers and widows

寡不敵眾
guǎ bù dí zhòng
be hopelessly outnumbered

寡廉鮮恥
guǎ lián xiǎn chǐ
shameless

沉默寡言
chén mò guǎ yán
uncommunicative; taciturn

失道寡助
shī dào guǎ zhù
An unjust cause finds scant support.

以寡敵眾
yí guǎ dí zhòng
pit a few against many; fight against heavy odds

Example:

她是一位孤寡老人。
Tā shì yíwèi gūguǎ lǎorén.
She is a lonely old lady.

guǎn

(close; shut)

Pictophonetic character, it is composed of 門, the symbol for door, on the outside and "絲", symbolising pieces of string, within. In ancient times, the door was made up of two wooden planks. After they were put together and tied with pieces of string, the door was securely shut.

關閉	guǎnbì	close; shut
關懷	guǎnhuái	show loving care for; show solicitude for
關鍵	guǎnjiàn	hinge; key; crux
關門	guǎnmén	close
關切	guǎnqiè	be deeply concerned; show one's concern over
關稅	guǎnshuì	customs duty; tariff
關係	guǎnxi	relation; relationship
關照	guǎnzhào	look after; keep an eye on

關懷備至
guān huái bèi zhì
show the utmost solicitude
關鍵時刻
guān jiàn shí kè
a critical (or crucial) moment
關門打狗
guān mén dǎ gǒu
bolt the door and beat the dog
i.e., block the enemy's retreat and then destroy him
緊要關頭
jǐn yào guān tóu
a critical moment
外交關係
wài jiāo guān xi
diplomatic relations

Example:

別把孩子整天關在家裡。
Bié bǎ háizi zhěng tiān guān zài jiālǐ.
Don't keep the children inside all day.

guān

(officials)

官

In metal language, "官" is composed of "宀" and "𠂤". The latter represents the masses while the former a house. Put together, they depict a house which is used for administering the people, i.e., an administration office or government building. By extension, this character has come to mean government officials.

官邸	guāndǐ	official residence; official mansion
官價	guānjià	official price (or rate)
官吏	guānlì	government officials
官僚	guānliáo	bureaucrat
官腔	guānqiāng	bureaucratic tone
官司	guānsi	lawsuit
官職	guānzhí	government post; official position

Chinese Made - Learning the Characters Through Illustrations

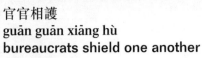

官官相護
guān guān xiāng hù
bureaucrats shield one another

官僚主義
guān liáo zhǔ yì
bureaucracy

官樣文章
guān yàng wén zhāng
mere formalities; officialese

官復原職
guān fù yuán zhí
restore an official to his original post; be reinstated

Example:

這人真官僚。
Zhè rén zhēn guānliáo.
What a bureaucrat that fellow is.

書畫叢中尋漢字

guó

(country; nation)

國

Ideogram. We find in oracle bones the initial form of this character "或", "戈" represents a dagger-axe, an ancient weapon; "o" a mouth and by extension people; and "▬" land. These were the three essential factors for the formation of a country, underlining the importance of protecting with arms the land and people from outside invasion. People in primitive society were pastoral and therefore their tribal organisations had no fixed territory or boundary. After many armed clashes, they gradually learned to set up defences around what they considered their land. By then, this character changed to "國" and still later to "國". Notice here the boundary is fixed; instead of with one side open, it is now closed. That is how the character for country is written now.

國寶	guóbǎo	national treasure
國賓	guóbīng	state guest
國萃	guócuì	the quintessence of Chinese culture
國恥	guóchǐ	national humiliation
國畫	guóhuà	traditional Chinese painting
國籍	guójí	nationality

74

國際貿易
guó jì mào yì
international trade
國計民生
guó jì mín shēng
the national economy and the people's livelihood
國際收支
guó jì shōu zhī
balance of (international) payments
國家元首
guó jiā yuán shǒu
head of state
國際主義
guó jì zhǔ yì
internationalism

Example:

在中國，婦女和兒童受國家保護。
Zài Zhōngguó, fùnǚ hé értóng shòu guójiā bǎohù.
In China, women and children are protected by the state.

guǒ

(fruit)

果

A pictogram indicating fruits grown on a tree. On oracle bones, it was written as "", which shows a tree with three fruits. In metal language, instead of three fruits "", there is only one, but it is much bigger "".

果斷	guǒduàn	resolute; decisive
果脯	guǒfǔ	preserved fruit; candied fruit
果敢	guǒgǎn	courageous and resolute
果醬	guǒjiàng	jam
果木	guǒmù	fruit tree
果然	guǒrán	really; as expected; sure enough
果真	guǒzhēn	really
果園	guǒyuán	orchard

辦事果斷
bàn shì guǒ duàn
handle affairs in a decisive manner

果實纍纍
guǒ shí lěi lěi
fruit growing in close clusters; fruit hanging heavy on the trees

果樹栽培
guǒ shù zāi péi
fruit growing; pomiculture

開花結果
kāi huā jiē guǒ
blossom and bear fruit

Example:

她果敢地跳入水中，救起溺水的孩子。
Tā guǒgǎn di tiào rù shuǐ zhōng, jiù qǐ nìshuǐ de háizi.
Without hesitation, she leapt into the water and saved the drowning child.

hán

(cold)

寒

The way this character "寒" looked in *Little Zhuan* was rather complicated. However, one can still distinguish its four components. A room or hut "冂", a haystack "茻", a man "仌" and ice "仌". From this combination, we can conclude that a man is sleeping in a haystack in a room, but underneath the haystack is ice. It must be very cold indeed.

寒潮	háncháo	cold current
寒磣	hánchen	ugly; unsightly
寒帶	hándài	frigid zone
寒流	hánliú	cold front
寒氣	hánqì	cold air; cold draught
寒酸	hánsuān	(of a poor scholar in the old days) miserable and shabby
寒心	hánxīn	be bitterly disappointed
寒衣	hányī	winter clothing
寒戰	hánzhàn	shiver (with cold or fear)

寒冬臘月
hán dōng là yuè
severe winter; dead of winter
寒風刺骨
hán fēng cì gǔ
The cold wind chilled one to the bone.
寒來暑往
hán lái shǔ wǎng
as summer goes and winter comes; with the passage of time
寒氣逼人
hán qì bī rén
There is a nip in the air.
天寒地凍
tiān hán dì dòng
The weather is cold and the ground is frozen.

Example:

初春季節仍有寒意。
Chūchūn jìjié réng yǒu hányì.
It's spring but there's still a chill in the air.

hé

(fit; combine)

合

In metal language, this ideogram looked like "合". The upper part is the lid of an urn or a pot "△", and the lower part the container itself "ᵾ". When the cover fits the pot, it means combine.

合抱	hébào	(of a tree, etc.) so big that one can just get one's arms around
合併	hébìng	merge; amalgamate
合唱	héchàng	chorus
合成	héchéng	compose; compound
合法	héfǎ	legal; lawful; legitimate; rightful
合格	hégé	qualified; up to standard
合歡	héhuān	silk tree
合理	hélǐ	rational; reasonable; equitable
合同	hétong	contract
合意	héyì	suit; be to one's liking (or taste)

合情合理
hé qíng hé lǐ
fair and reasonable; fair and sensible
合影留念
hé yǐng liú niàn
have a group photo taken to mark the occasion
合作經濟
hé zuò jīng jì
cooperative economy; cooperative sector of the economy
合二而一
hé èr ér yī
two combine into one

Example:

這幅畫是他們合作的。
Zhèi fú huà shì tāmen hézuò de.
This painting is their joint work.

hè

(festive; congratulatory)

賀

Pictophonetic character composed of 加 and 貝. The top part means to increase, and the lower part is the symbol for shell, which was the currency used in primitive society. When one already has plenty of money, and one's friends and relatives come along with gifts, that increases his belongings. Hence a festive or congratulatory occasion.

賀詞	hècí	speech (or message) of congratulation; congratulations; greetings
賀電	hèdiàn	message of congratulation; congratulatory telegram
賀禮	hèlǐ	gift (as a token of congratulation)
賀年	hènián	extend New Year greetings or pay a New Year call
賀喜	hèxǐ	congratulate sb. on a happy occasion (e.g. a wedding, the birth of a child, etc.)
賀信	hèxìn	letter of congratulation

恭賀新禧
gōng hè xīn xǐ
Happy New Year
慶賀新年
qìng hè xīn nián
to greet or celebrate the New Year

Example:

我對你的成功致以最熱烈的祝賀。
Wǒ duì nǐ de chénggōng zhì yǐ zuì rèliè de zhùhè.
I send you my warmest congratulations on your success.

hui

(ash)

灰

In metal language, this ideogram was written as "灵". A hand "彐" on top and a fire "火" below, indicating the act of taking something out of the fire. When you pick something out from a fire, you don't want to burn yourself. You have to wait for the fire to die out. By that time all that is left are the ashes.

灰暗	huī'àn	murky grey; gloomy
灰白	huībái	greyish white; ashen; pale
灰色	huīsè	grey; ashy; pessimistic; gloomy
灰心	huīxīn	lost heart; be discouraged
灰溜溜	huīliūliū	gloomy; dejected; crestfallen
灰蒙蒙	huīméngméng	dusky; overcast

灰心喪氣
huī xīn sàng qì
be utterly disheartened

化為灰燼
huà wéi huī jìn
be reduced to ashes

心灰意懶
xīn huī yì lǎn
fell disheartened

成功不驕傲，失敗不灰心
chéng gōng bù jiāo'ào, shī bài bù huī xīn
when you succeed don't get conceited; when you fail don't be dejected

Example:

大風過後，桌子上落了一層灰。
Dàfēng guò hòu, zhuōzi shang luò le yìcéng huī.
After the wind, there was a layer of dust on the desk.

jiān

(scrutinise)

監

An ideogram. In metal language, it was written as "囧". The sign on the upper left, "臣", signifies a wide-open eye, "ㄱ" on the upper right a person bent low and looking downward, "ㅛ" in the lower half represents a vessel, and the horizontal line "●" above it indicates that it is filled to the brim with water. We now know that the primitive people used water as their mirror. The original meaning of this character then was looking down into the water to examine oneself. Now it means to look at other people closely or to scrutinise.

監察	jiānchá	supervise, control
監犯	jiānfàn	prisoner; convict
監護	jiānhù	guardianship
監考	jiānkǎo	invigilate
監牢	jiānláo	prison; jail
監票	jiānpiào	scrutinise balloting
監視	jiānshì	keep watch on; keep a lookout over
監聽	jiāntīng	monitor

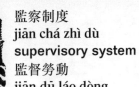

監察制度
jiān chá zhì dù
supervisory system

監督勞動
jiān dū láo dòng
do penal labour under surveillance

監守自盜
jiān shǒu zì dào
steal what is entrusted to one's care; embezzle

Example:

有一位警察在房外監視。
Yǒu yíwèi jǐngchá zài fángwài jiānshì.
There is a policeman watching outside the house.

書畫叢中尋漢字

jiǎng

(border; boundary)

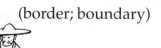

疆

A pictogram consisting of three parts: 弓, 土 and "畺". 土 is earth or land, 弓 is an instrument to measure the land, and "畺" is composed of three horizontal lines separating the two farmland symbols. Hence the meaning: border or boundary.

疆場	jiǎngchǎng	battlefield
疆界	jiǎngjiè	boundary; border
疆土	jiǎngtǔ	territory
疆域	jiǎngyù	territory; domain

馳騁疆場
chí chéng jiāng chǎng
demonstrate one's bravery on battlefield

駐守邊疆
zhù shǒu biān jiāng
stationed on the frontier

Example:

保衛國家疆土完整，是軍人的神聖職責。
Bǎowèi guójiā jiāng tǔ wánzhěng, shì jūnrén de zhénshèng zhízé.
It is the sacred duty of a soldier to safeguard the nation's territorial integrity.

jiāo

(proud; arrogant)

驕

Pictogram. The left part is a horse while the right is a verb meaning to lift high. The original meaning of this character was a horse raising its head high or an untamed horse. From that it was extended to mean being arrogant.

驕傲	jiāo'ào	arrogant; conceited
驕橫	jiāohéng	arrogant and imperious; overbearing
驕矜	jiāojīn	self-important; proud; haughty
驕氣	jiāoqi	overbearing airs; arrogance
驕縱	jiāozòng	arrogant and wilful

驕傲自大
jiāo ào zì dà
swollen with pride; conceited and arrogant

驕兵必敗
jiāo bīng bì bài
An army puffed up with pride is bound to lose.

驕陽似火
jiāo yáng sì huǒ
scorching sun

驕奢淫逸
jiāo shē yín yì
lordly, luxury-loving and wallowing in luxury and pleasure

勝不驕，敗不餒
shèng bù jiāo, bài bù něi
not be dizzy with success, nor discourage by failure

Example:

她為人謙遜，毫無驕矜之態。
Tā wéirén qiānxùn, háowú jiāojīn zhītài.
She is modest, and never puts on airs.

書畫叢中尋漢字

jiě
(separate; dissect)

解

An ideogram composed of 角(horn), 牛(ox) and 刀(knife). To cut off the horn of an ox with a knife is to dissect, cut apart or separate.

解饞	jiěchán	satisfy a craving for good food
解答	jiědá	answer; explain
解恨	jiěhèn	vent one's hatred; have one's hatred slaked
解決	jiějué	solve; resolve; settle
解渴	jiěkě	quench one's thirst
解釋	jiěshì	explain; expound; interpret
解說	jiěshuō	explain orally; comment
解脫	jiětuō	free (or extricate) oneself

解除婚約
jiě chú hūn yuē
renounce an engagement

解放思想
jiě fàng sī xiǎng
emancipate the mind; free oneself from old ideas

解決爭端
jiě jué zhēng duān
settle a dispute

解鈴繫鈴
jiě líng xì líng
let him who tied the bell on the tiger take it off

i.e., whoever started the trouble should end it

解囊相助
jiě náng xiāng zhù
help sb. generously with money

Example:

這西瓜真解渴。
Zhè xīguā zhēn jiěkě.
This watermelon really quenches your thrist.

93

jìn
(clean up; exhaust;
to the utmost)

盡

From oracle bones, we find the origin of this character which consists of three parts "". At the bottom is a vessel "", on top is a hand "", and in the middle, a brush "". Holding a brush to clean a vessel, that is the original meaning of this pictogram.

盡力	**jìnlì**	**do all one can; try one's best**
盡量	**jìnliàng**	**(drink or eat) to the full; try one's best**
盡情	**jìnqíng**	**to one's heart's content; as much as one likes**
盡是	**jìnshì**	**full of; all; without exception**
盡頭	**jìntóu**	**end**
盡興	**jìnxìng**	**to one's heart's content; enjoy oneself to the full**
盡職	**jìnzhí**	**fulfil one's duty**
盡義務	**jìnyìwù**	**do one's duty; fulfil one's obligation**

盡人皆知
jìn rén jiē zhī
be known to all; be common knowledge

盡情歡呼
jìn qíng huān hū
cheer heartily

盡善盡美
jìn shàn jìn měi
the acme of perfection; perfect

盡收眼底
jìn shōu yǎn dǐ
have a panoramic view

盡心竭力
jìn xīn jié lì
(do sth.) with all one's heart and all one's might

一言難盡
yì yán nán jìn
It can't be expressed in a few words.

Example:

他工作一向很盡職。
Tā gōngzuò yíxiàng hěn jìnzhí.
He has always been a conscientious worker.

書畫叢中尋漢字

jǐng

(a well)

井

In metal language, this pictogram was written as "井", indicting a big hole on the ground with boards placed around it forming a square. The dot in the middle represents the water inside.

井壁	jǐngbì	wall of a well
井場	jǐngchǎng	well site
井底	jǐngdǐ	the bottom of a well
井架	jǐngjià	derrick
井口	jǐngkǒu	the mouth of a well; pithead; wellhead
井然	jǐngrán	orderly; neat and tidy; shipshape, methodical
井筒	jǐngtǒng	pit shaft
井鹽	jǐngyán	well salt

井底之蛙
jǐng dǐ zhi wā
a frog in a well

i.e., a person with a very limited outlook

井井有條
jǐng jǐng yǒu tiáo
in perfect order; shipshape; methodical

秩序井然
zhì xù jǐng rán
in good order

井水不犯河水
jǐng shuǐ bú fàn hé shuǐ
well water does not intrude into river water

i.e., I'll mind my own business, you mind yours.

Example:

中國有句俗話叫做：吃水不忘挖井人。

Zhōngguó yǒu jù súhuà jiào zuò: chī shuǐ bú wàng wā jǐng rén.

We Chinese have an adage: "When you drink the water, remember those who dug the well."

jū

(reside; residence)

居

In ancient times, " 尸 ", the upper part of this character, referred to a person's buttock while 古, the lower part, meant staying put. To have one's buttock stay put in a place for an extended period is to reside.

居多	jūduō	be in the majority
居功	jūgōng	claim credit for oneself
居留	jūliú	reside
居民	jūmín	resident; inhabitant
居然	jūrán	unexpectedly; to one's surprise
居士	jūshì	lay Buddhist
居住	jūzhù	live; reside; dwell

居高臨下
jū gāo lín xià
occupy a commanding position (or height)

居功自傲
jū gōng zì ào
claim credit for oneself and become arrogant

居間調停
jū jiān tiáo tíng
mediate between two parties; act as mediator

居心不良
jū xīn bù liáng
harbour evil intentions

居中斡旋
jū zhōng wò xuán
mediate between disputants; be placed in the middle

居安思危
jū ān sī wēi
be prepared for danger in times of peace; be vigilant in peace time

Example:

你怎麼居然相信這種謠言。
Nǐ zěnmo jūrán xiāngxìn zhèizhǒng yáoyán?
How could you believe such a rumour?

jūn

(ruler; sovereign)

君

In metal language, it was written as "㞷". The top part, "㞷" represents a hand holding a power stick and the lower part "ᵕ" a mouth. He who holds a power stick and orders people around is obviously a ruler. Later on, the character evolved to mean a sovereign.

君遷子	jūnqiānzǐ	the fruit of date plum (*Diospyros lotus*)
君權	jūnquán	monarchical power
君主	jūnzhǔ	monarch; sovereign
君子	jūnzǐ	a man of noble character; gentleman
諸君	zhùjūn	friends; gentlemen; ladies and gentlemen (a way of addressing a group)

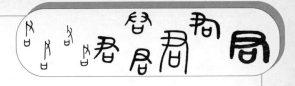

正人君子
zhèng rén jūn zǐ
a man of moral integrity

君主立憲
jūn zhǔ lì xiàn
constitutional monarchy

君主專制
jūn zhǔ zhuān zhì
autocratic monarchy; absolute monarchy

君子成人之美
jūn zǐ chéng rén zhī měi
A gentleman is always ready to help others attain their aims.

以小人之心，度君子之腹
Yǐ xiǎo rén zhī xīn, dù jūn zǐ zhī fù.
gauge the heart of a gentleman with one's own mean measure

Example:

來訪者乃君主本人。
Lǎi fǎng zhě nǎi jūnzhǔ běnrén.
The visitor was none other than the monarch himself.

書畫叢中尋漢字

jūn

(troop; army)

軍

In ancient times, chariots were the vehicle used by warriors when they fought a battle while carts were the chief means of transportation. The chariots were also used as ramparts to protect the bivouac when troops on the march stopped overnight to rest. Hence the character "軍", which shows the character "車" being encircled. The "◯" sign later evolved into "⌒", and the character came to mean the army itself.

軍備	jūnbèi	armament; arms
軍方	jūnfāng	the military
軍官	jūnguān	officer
軍火	jūnhuǒ	munitions; arms and ammunition
軍醫	jūnyī	medical officer; military surgeon
軍營	jūnyíng	military camp; barracks
軍職	jūnzhí	official post in the army; military appointment
軍裝	jūnzhuāng	military (or army) uniform; uniform

軍備競賽
jūn bèi jìng sài
armament (or arms) race

軍法審判
jūn fǎ shěn pàn
court-martial

軍閥戰爭
jūn fá zhàn zhēng
war among warlords

軍事訓練
jūn shì xùn liàn
military training

軍銜制度
jūn xián zhì dù
system of military ranks

軍心大振
jūn xīn dà zhèn
The morale of the troops has been greatly raised.

Example:

他的軍齡比我長。
Tā de jūnlíng bǐ wǒ cháng.
He has served in the army longer than I have.

書畫叢中尋漢字

kòu
(bandit; intruder)

寇

In metal language, this ideogram "寇" reveals its meaning right away. Its upper part "冖" represents a house or a room, "𠂊" the shape of a man with a protruding head and "𠬝" his hand holding a weapon. The combination depicts a man with a weapon sneaking into a house. Hence an intruder, or a bandit.

寇仇	kòuchóu	enemy; foe
海寇	hǎikòu	pirate
敵寇	díkòu	the (invading) enemy
入寇	rùkòu	invade (a country)

勝者為王，敗者為寇

shèng zhě wéi wáng, bài zhě wéi kòu

He who wins becomes the king; he who loses

becomes the bandit; history is written by the winners.

寇準背靴

Kòuzhǔn bēi xuē

"Kou Zun Carries His Boots," name of a Peking Opera about a Song Dynasty prime minister

Example:

他們勇敢地抵抗兇殘的敵寇。

Tāmen yǒnggǎn di dǐkàng xiōngcán de díkòu.

They stood up to the cruel enemy.

lǐ
(ceremomy;
etiquette; rites)

禮

On the left is the character 示 which means praying or presenting offerings before an altar. On the right is the character "豊", which is another version of "豐", meaning abundant or sumptuous, its lower part "豆" representing a long-legged plate and the upper part "曲", the offerings. That was the original meaning. Now it has come to mean rituals or ceremony in general.

禮拜	lǐbài	religious service
禮服	lǐfú	ceremonial robe; formal attire
禮花	lǐhuā	fireworks display
禮教	lǐjiào	the Confucian or feudal ethical code
禮貌	lǐmào	courtesy; politeness; manners
禮品	lǐpǐn	gift; present
禮物	lǐwù	gift; present

禮尚往來
lǐ shàng wǎng lái
courtesy demands reciprocity

彬彬有禮
bīn bīn yǒu lǐ
refined and courteous

社交禮節
shè jiāo lǐ jié
social etiquette

禮輕人意重
lǐ qīng rén yì zhòng
The gift is trifling but the feeling is profound; it's nothing much, but it's the thought that counts.

Example:

這是禮節上所需要的。
Zhèshì lǐjié shang suǒ xūyào de.
This is required by protocol.

107

lì
(stand)

立

Pictogram. In metal language it was "立". Its upper part "大" represents a person with arms and legs out-stretched. Beneath it a horizontal line, meaning the ground. Surely when a person is doing that, he or she is standing and not sitting.

立案	lì'àn	register; put on record
立場	lìchǎng	position; stand; standpoint
立功	lìgōng	render meritorious service; do a deed of merit; win honour; make contributions
立櫃	lìguì	clothes closet; wardrobe; hanging cupboard
立即	lìjí	immediately; at once; promptly
立誓	lìshì	take an oath; vow
立體	lìtǐ	three-dimensional; stereoscopic
立足點	lìzúdiǎn	foothold; footing

立場堅定
lì chǎng jiān dìng
be steadfast in one's stand; take a firm stand

立見功效
lì jiàn gōng xiào
produce immediate results; feel the effect immediately

立候回音
lì hòu huí yīn
An immediate reply is requested.

立竿見影
lì gān jiàn yǐng
set up a pole and see its shadow

i.e., get instant results

立錐之地
lì zhuī zhī dì
a place to stick an awl

i.e., a tiny bit of land

立於不敗之地
lì yú bú bài zhī dì
establish oneself in an unassailable position; remain invincible; be in an impregnable position

Example:

這幅畫立意新穎。
Zhèi fú huà lìyì xīnyǐng.
This painting shows an interesting new approach.

lì 麗

(beauty; pairing)

Pictogram. In metal language it looks like this: "𪋙". The lower part "𪊽" is a deer and the upper part "䚙" its two large spreading horns. The combination means, by extension, beauty or forming company.

麗人	lìrén	a beauty
附麗	fùlì	depend on; attach oneself to
美麗	měilì	beautiful
秀麗	xiùlì	pretty; graceful; elegant
壯麗	zhuànglì	magnificent; majestic
佳麗	jiālì	beautiful women

風和日麗
fēng hé rì lì
The wind is gentle and the sun radiant.

天生麗質
tiān shēng lì zhì
natural beauty

山河壯麗
shān hé zhuàng lì
a country's majestic scenery; beauty of the landscape

無所附麗
wú suǒ fù lì
no one to depend on

麗人如雲
lì rén rú yún
beauties are numerous like clouds

Example:

她既美麗又聰明。
Tā jì měilì yòu cōngming.
Her beauty equals her intelligence.

lì
(experience; history;
calendar)

The same character on oracle bones, " 秼 ", had two " 秝 " signs on top is the generic term for farm produce. The symbol at the bottom " 屮 " represents the foot. Someone who leaves his footprints on large tracts of land is certainly well travelled and experienced. By extension, the character also means history, calendar.

歷程	lìchéng	course
歷次	lìcì	all previous
歷代	lìdài	successive dynasties
歷年	lìnián	over the years
歷任	lìrèn	have successively held the posts of
歷史	lìshǐ	history
歷數	lìshǔ	count one by one

歷盡艱辛
lì jìn jiān xīn
experienced all kinds of hardship
歷代名畫
lì dài míng huà
famous paintings through the ages
歷歷在目
lì lì zài mù
come clearly into view, leap up vividly before the eyes
歷史潮流
lì shǐ cháo liú
the tide of history; historical trend

Example:

在歷次比賽中她都取得了優異的成績。
Zài lìcì bǐsài zhōng tā dōu qǔdé le yōuyì de chéngjì.
She has done well in all past contests.

113

liǎng
(a measurement
unit; a pair)

From the metal language version "", we can see that the original meaning of this ideogram was two persons side by side, i.e., a pair. This character was later used as a measurement unit. One *liang* equals one-tenth of a *catty*, which is half a kilo.

兩邊	liǎngbiān	both sides; both directions; both places
兩便	liǎngbiàn	be convenient to both; make things easy for both
兩極	liǎngjí	the two poles of the earth; the two poles (of a magnet or an electric battery)
兩面	liǎngmiàn	two sides; both sides; two aspects
兩難	liǎngnán	face a difficult choice; be in a dilemma
兩手	liǎngshǒu	dual tactics
兩性	liǎngxìng	both sexes
兩樣	liǎngyàng	different

Chinese Made - *Learning the Characters Through Illustrations*

兩敗俱傷
liǎng bài jù shāng
both sides suffer (or lose); neither side gains

兩面三刀
liǎng miàn sān dāo
double-dealing

兩全其美
liǎng quán qí měi
satisfy both sides; satisfy rival claims

兩廂情願
liǎng xiāng qíng yuàn
both parties are willing

兩袖清風
liǎng xiù qīng fēng
(of an official) have clean hands; remain uncorrupted

兩面夾攻
liǎng miàn jiā gōng
make a pincer attack; be caught in cross fire; be caught in a pincer attack

兩耳不聞窗外事
liǎng ěr bù wén chuāng wài shì
not care what is going on outside one's window

i.e., be oblivious of the outside world

Example:

這張紙兩面都寫滿了字。
Zhèi zhāng zhǐ liǎngmiàn dōu xiě mǎn le zì.
This piece of paper is covered with writing on both sides.

書畫叢中尋漢字

mào

(emit; prop up)

Pictogram. The ancient version of this character "𡨂" looked like a person with a head cover, but with his or her eyes "⊖" exposed. So the headgear for children came to be called " 冒 " (for adults it was called *guan* 冠). Later, as the character also took on the meaning of "emit" and "crop up", a " 巾 " was added to 帽 for hats in general.

冒充	màochōng	pretend to be (sb. or sth. else); pass sb. or sth. off as
冒犯	màofàn	offend; affront
冒火	màohuǒ	burn with anger; get angry; flare up
冒昧	màomèi	make bold; venture; take the liberty
冒牌	màopái	a counterfeit of a well-known trade mark; imitation
冒失	màoshi	rash; abrupt
冒險	màoxiǎn	take a risk; take chances

冒充内行
mào chōng nèi háng
pretend to be an expert; pose as an expert

冒犯禁令
mào fàn jìn lìng
violate a prohibition

冒昧陳辭
mào mèi chén cí
make bold to express my views; venture an opinion

冒天下之大不韙
mào tiān xià zhi dà bù wěi
defy world opinion; risk universal condemnation; fly in the face of the will of the people

Example:

她就愛冒險。
Tā jiù ài màoxiǎn.
She likes to take risks.

書畫叢中尋漢字

měi

(beautiful; delicious)

美

An ideogram consisting of 羊 and 大. In metal language, it was "美", with the upper part "羊" looking like a sheep, and the lower part "大" meaning big, indicating a big, fat sheep which tastes delicious. Later the character evolved to mean delicious or beautiful.

美稱	měichēng	laudatory title; good name
美德	měidé	virtue; moral excellence
美感	měigǎn	aesthetic feeling; aesthetic perception; sense of beauty
美觀	měiguān	pleasing to the eye; beautiful; artistic
美好	měihǎo	fine; happy; glorious
美夢	měimèng	fond dream
美妙	měimiào	beautiful; splendid; wonderful
美術	měishù	the fine arts; art

美滿婚姻
měi mǎn hūn yīn
happy marriage; conjugal happiness
美其名曰
měi qí míng yuē
call it by the fine-sounding name of
美術設計
měi shù shè jì
artistic design
美味小吃
měi wèi xiǎo chī
dainty snacks
美不勝收
měi bú shèng shōu
so many beautiful things that one simply can't take them all in
美中不足
měi zhōng bù zú
a blemish in an otherwise perfect thing; a fly in the ointment

Example:

瞧他這美勁兒。
Qiáo tā zhè měijìnr.
Look how pleased he is with himself.

míng

(name)

名

In metal language, this ideogram was written as "名". The upper part "夕" represents night, so dark one cannot distinguish the face of someone nearby. The mouth sign "口" underneath implies that one has to ask who that person is. Together, they convey the idea of telling someone else one's own name or inquiring about the other's name.

名詞	míngcí	noun; substantive; term; phrase
名單	míngdān	name list
名貴	míngguì	famous and precious; rare
名家	míngjiā	the School of Logicians (in the Spring and Autumn and Warring States Periods, 770-221 B.C.); a person of academic or artistic distinction; famous expert; master
名將	míngjiàng	famous general; great soldier
名流	míngliú	distinguished personages; celebrities
名聲	míngshēng	reputation; repute; renown
名著	míngzhù	famous book; famous work

Chinese Made - Learning the Characters Through Illustrations

名山大川
míng shān dà chuān
famous mountains and great rivers

名正言順
míng zhèng yán shùn
come within one's jurisdiction; be perfectly justifiable

名不副實
míng bù fù shí
the name falls short of the reality; be sth. more in name than in reality; be unworthy of the name or title

名不虛傳
míng bù xū chuán
have a well-deserved reputation; deserve the reputation one enjoys; live up to one's reputation

名存實亡
míng cún shí wáng
cease to exist except in name; exist in name only

名副其實
míng fù qí shí
the name matches the reality; be sth. in reality as well as in name; be worthy of the name

名列前茅
míng liè qián máo
be among the best of the successful candidates

Example:

這種花的名字很特別。
Zhèi zhǒng huā de míngzi hěn tèbié.
This flower has a peculiar name.

míng

(bright; clear)

This pictogram was written as "☽ / ◑" in metal language. On the left is " ☉ " (the sun), or " ⊘ " (window), and on the right "☽ / ☽" (moon). Put together, they indicate that thanks to the sun and moon coming in through the window, the room is well lit. Hence brightness.

明暗	míng'àn	light and shade
明白	míngbai	clear; obvious; plain; frank; unequivocal, explicit
明暢	míngchàng	lucid and smooth
明澈	míngchè	bright and limpid; transparent
明斷	míngduàn	pass (fair) judgment
明朗	mínglǎng	bright and clear; obvious; forthright; bright an cheerful
明媚	míngmèi	bright and beautiful; radiant and enchanting
明星	míngxīng	star

明目張膽
míng mù zhāng dǎn
brazenly; flagrantly

明哲保身
míng zhé bǎo shēn
be worldly wise and play safe

明爭暗鬥
míng zhēng àn dòu
both open strife and veiled struggle

明辨是非
míng biàn shì fēi
make a clear distinction between right and wrong

明知故犯
míng zhī gù fàn
knowingly violate (discipline, etc.); deliberately break (a rule, etc.); do sth. one knows is wrong

明知故問
míng zhī gù wèn
ask a question while knowing the answer

明槍易躲，暗箭難防
míng qiāng yì duǒ, àn jiàn nán fáng
It is easy to dodge a spear shot in the open, but hard to guard against an arrow from a hidden corner.

Example:

他這樣決定是明智的。
Tā zhèyàng juédìng shì míngzhì de.
It was wise of him to make that decision.

書畫叢中尋漢字

mǔ

(mother)

母

Originally, this pictogram was written as "", indicating a woman with two big nipples, clearly distinguishing women who are married and have children from those who are unmarried or married but without children.

母愛	mǔ'ài	mother love; maternal love
母機	mǔjī	machine tool; mother aircraft; launching aircraft
母親	mǔqīn	mother
母校	mǔxiào	one's old school; Alma Mater
母性	mǔxìng	maternal instinct
母語	mǔyǔ	mother tongue
母老虎	mǔlǎohǔ	tigress; vixen; shrew

母本植株
mǔ běn zhí zhù
maternal plant

母系親屬
mǔ xì qīn shǔ
maternal relatives

母系社會
mǔ xì shè huì
matriarchal society

失敗是成功之母
Shī bài shì chéng gōng zhī mǔ.
Failure is the mother of success.

Example:

她像母親一樣對待那些可憐的流浪兒童。
Tā xiàng mǔqīn yíyàng duìdài nàxie kělián de liúlàng értóng.
She was like a mother to the poor waifs.

ní
(nun)

尼

From the oracle bones "", we see two persons close to each other, in fact one with his back against the other's front. That was the original meaning of the character 尼 (also 昵). The expression 尼姑 or 比丘尼 is the transliteration of the Sanskrit word "Bhiksuni," which means a nun of the Buddhist faith.

尼庵	ní'ān	Buddhist nunnery
尼姑	nígū	Buddhist nun
尼龍	nílóng	nylon
尼古丁	nígǔdīng	nicotine
尼羅河	Níluóhé	the Nile

126

削髮為尼
xuē fà wéi ní
becomes a nun
尼羅河慘案
Níluǒhé Cǎn'àn
"Death on the Nile," a famous crime story by Agatha Christie
尼亞加拉瀑布
Níyajiālā Pùbù
Niagara Falls

Example:

他穿了一件尼龍做的衣服。
Tā chuān le yíjiàn nílóng zuò de yīfu.
He wore a dress of nylon.

nián

(year)

年

Pictogram. In oracle bones, 年 was " 秂 ". The lower part is a man " 丿 "; on his head is an ear of wheat or rice " 𠂉 ", and " 禾 " represents harvest. In ancient China, farmers harvested one crop a year. As the year drew to a close, they would make offerings to their ancestors. That is why 年 is represented by a person with wheat or rice ears on his head as the symbol of the annual offerings.

年代	niándài	age; years; time; a decade of a century
年底	niándǐ	the end of the year
年糕	niángāo	New Year cake (made of glutinous rice flour)
年關	niánguān	the end of the year (formerly time for settling accounts)
年華	niánhuá	time; years
年貨	niánhuò	special purchases for the Spring Festival
年景	niánjǐng	the year's harvest
年輪	niánlún	annual ring; growth ring

Chinese Made - Learning the Characters Through Illustrations

年富力強
nián fù lì qiáng
in the prime of life; in one's prime

年復一年
nián fù yì nián
year after year; year in year out; annually

年高德劭
nián gāo dé shào
of venerable age and eminent virtue; venerable

年深日久
nián shēn rì jiǔ
with the passage of time; as the years go by

虛度年華
xū dù nián huá
idle away one's time; waste one's life

Example:

年代久了，石碑上的字跡已經模糊了。
Niándài jiǔ le, shíbēi shang de zìjì yǐjing móhu le.
The inscriptions on the stone tablet have become blurred with the passage of time.

書畫叢中尋漢字

qī
(wife)

妻

In metal language, the ideogram looked much more complicated than now "𢆶". The lower part "𢀖" represents a woman, who is using her hand "彐" to put hairpins "ψ" on her head. This is the kind of hairdo a woman wears during her wedding ceremony to indicate she is going to be the wife of a man.

妻孥	qīnú	wife and children
妻子	qīzǐ	wife and children
妻子	qīzi	wife
妻女	qīnǚ	the women of the family
人妻	rénqī	wife

Chinese Made - *Learning the Characters Through Illustrations*

妻兒老小
qī ér lǎo xiǎo
a married man's entire family
i.e., parents, wife and children
妻離子散
qī lí zǐ sàn
breaking up or scattering of one's family
結髮夫妻
jié fà fū qī
a married couple
妻憑夫貴
qī píng fū guì
The wife's status grows with her husband's rise in position and power.

Example:

她一定會成為一個好妻子。
Tā yídìng huì chéngwéi yígè hǎo qīzi.
She will make a good wife.

131

qiè

(concubine)

妾

In *Little Zhuan*, the character was written as " 妾 ". The upper part " 立 " is the symbol of a torture knife, which implies that a criminal is under punishment. The lower part " 女 " represents a woman. Put together, they refer to a female prisoner of war or slave. Gradually, this ideogram evolved to mean a man's concubine.

| 納妾 | nàqiè | tak a concubine |
| 妻妾 | qīqiè | wife and concubine(s) |

Chinese Made - *Learning the Characters Through Illustrations*

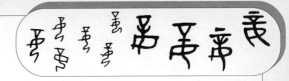

三妻六妾
sān qī liù qiè
three wives and six concubines

(meaning many of them)
妻妾成群
qī qiè chéng qùn
a flock of wives and concubines

Example:

世界上仍有少數國家允許納妾。
Shìjiè shang rěng yǒu shǎoshù guójiā yǔnxǔ nàqiè.
There are in the world still a few countries which allow people to have concubines.

qìng
(festivities;
celebration)

慶

Originally, 慶 was written as "慶". The upper part "𢉠" is half of the character for deer, the middle part was "心" for heart and the lower part "夂" for feet. What this character tries to convey is a man carrying a deer on his back to present to his loved one. Hence the meaning: happiness and festivities.

慶典	qìngdiǎn	celebration; a ceremony to celebrate
慶賀	qìnghè	congratulate; celebrate
慶幸	qìngxìng	rejoice
慶祝	qìngzhù	celebrate
慶功會	qìnggōng huì	victory meeting

慶祝國慶
qìng zhù guó qìng
celebrate National Day
慶祝大會
qìng zhù dà huì
celebration meeting
盛大慶典
shèng dà qìng diǎn
grand celebrations
慶父不死，魯難未已
Qìng fù bù sǐ, Lǔ nán wèi yǐ
Until Qing Fu is done away with, the crisis in the state of Lu will not be over.

i.e., There will always be trouble until he who stirs it up is removed.

Example:

我慶幸自己死裡逃生。
Wǒ qìngxìng zìjǐ sǐ lǐ táo shēng.
I congratulate myself on my narrow escape.

quán
(spring;
fountain)

泉

In oracle bones, it was written as "𤽄". "𣲗" is the symbol of a running stream and "𠂆" that of the surrounding mountains. This ideogram suggests water coming out from a cave or opening in the mountain. In other words, a spring or fountain.

泉水	quánshuǐ	spring water; spring
泉眼	quányǎn	the mouth of a spring; spring
泉源	quányuán	fountainhead; springhead; wellspring; source
溫泉	wēnquán	hot spring
礦泉	kuàngquán	mineral spring
噴泉	pēnquán	fountain

Chinese Made - *Learning the Characters Through Illustrations*

淚如泉湧
lèi rú quán yǒng
tears well up in one's eyes

湧泉潺潺
yǒng quán chán chán
the bubbling of the spring

智慧的源泉
zhì huì de yuán quán
source of wisdom

力量的源泉
lì liang de yuán quán
source of strength

Example:

這地方因溫泉而出名。
Zhèi dìfang yīn wēnquán ér chūmíng.
The place is famous for its hot springs.

rán

(burn; ignite)

然

In *Little Zhuan*, the character was written as "🔥". "𣍐" on the upper left represents flesh, "犬" on the upper right a dog and "火" down below a fire. The original meaning of this character was to barbecue dog's meat. Now it has taken on quite a different meaning.

然而	rán'ér	yet; but; however
然後	ránhòu	then; after that; afterwards
然諾	ránnuò	promise; pledge
然則	ránzé	in that case; then
忽然	hūrán	suddenly; all of a sudden
顯然	xiǎnrán	obviously

不以為然
bù yǐ wéi rán
object to; not approve

大謬不然
dà miù bù rán
entirely wrong; absurd

巍然屹立
wēi rán yì lì
tower majestically

知其然，不知其所以然
zhī qí rán, bù zhī qí suǒ yǐ rán
know the hows but not the whys

Example:

試驗失敗了多次，然而他們並不灰心。
Shíyàn shībài le duōcì, rán'ér tāmen bìng bù huīxīn.
Time after time they failed in the experiment, but they didn't lose heart.

rén
(humanity;
benevolence)

An ideogram with two components. On the left side is " 亻", the radical for humans, and on the right side are two horizontal lines " 二 " implying two individuals. Together they refer to what governs human relationship, in other words, love and humanity. 仁 is one of the basic tenets of Confucianism.

仁愛	rén'ài	kindheartedness
仁慈	réncí	benevolent; merciful; kind
仁兄	rénxiōng	my dear friend
仁政	rénzhèng	policy of benevolence; benevolent government

仁人志士
rén rén zhì shì
people with lofty ideals
仁義道德
rén yì dào dé
humanity, justice and virtue; virtue and morality
仁至義盡
rén zhì yì jìn
do everything called for by humanity and duty; do what is humanly possible to help;
show extreme forbearance
麻木不仁
má mù bù rén
insensitive; apathetic
仁者見仁，智者見智
rén zhě jiàn rén, zhì zhě jiàn zhì
the benevolent see benevolence and the wise see wisdon
i.e., different people have different views

Example:

我們對這些人，真可謂到了仁至義盡。
Wǒmen duì zhèixiē rén zhēn kěwèi dào le rén zhì yì jìn.
We have really shown the utmost tolerance and patience towards these people.

róng

(to flourish; glory; prosperity)

In metal language, "" looked like two crossed flower stems or ears of wheat. It conveyed a flourishing picture. Hence the meaning to flourish. The character has evolved to mean glory and prosperity too.

榮歸	rónggui	return in glory
榮獲	rónghuò	have the honour to get or win
榮軍	róngjūn	disabled soldier (wounded in revolutionary war)
榮辱	róngrǔ	honour or disgrace
榮幸	róngxìng	be honoured
榮譽	róngyù	honour; credit; glory

榮歸故里
róng guī gù lǐ
return to one's native place with honour

榮華富貴
róng huá fù guì
glory; splendour, wealth and rank; high position and great wealth

榮辱與共
róng rǔ yǔ gòng
share weal and woe

榮譽稱號
róng yù chēng hào
honorary titles

春榮冬枯
chūn róng dōng kū
grow in spring and wither in winter

欣欣向榮
xīn xīn xiàng róng
flourishing; thriving; growing luxuriantly

Example:

今天很榮幸能參加你們的晚會。
Jīntiān hěn róngxìng néng cānjiā nǐmen de wǎnhuì.
It is a great honour to be with you at this evening party.

ruò

(as if)

若

In oracle bones, this pictogram was written as " 𦭓 " with the middle part " 𦫦 " indicating a person with long hair, the symbols " 𠂇 " and " 彐 " on both sides representing her two hands raised to arrange her hair. That was the original meaning of this character. Now it means something quite different.

若蟲	ruòchóng	nymph
若非	ruòfēi	if not; were it not for
若干	ruògān	certain number or amount; how many; how much
若是	ruòshì	if

Chinese Made - Learning the Characters Through Illustrations

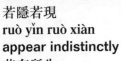

若隱若現
ruò yǐn ruò xiàn
appear indistinctly

若有所失
ruò yǒu suǒ shī
feel as if something were missing; look distracted

若即若離
ruò jí ruò lí
be neither friendly nor aloof; maintain a lukewarm relationship; keep sb. at arm's length

若明若暗
ruò míng ruò àn
have an indistinct (or blurred) picture of; have a hazy (or vague) notion about

Example:

若非親身經歷，豈知其中甘苦。
Ruò fēi qīnshēn jīnglì, qǐ zhī qízhōng gānkǔ.
You cannot appreciate the difficulty except through personal experience.

書畫叢中尋漢字

shàn
(good;
virtuous)

善

The original form of this ideogram looked very complicated "善". The top part is the character for sheep 羊, with two symbols for speak "誩" below it. 羊 is also equivalent to 祥, which means auspicious. The combination of two speak symbols indicate that there are more than one person speaking. There is a Chinese saying, "Listen to both sides and you will be enlightened." Such a conversation as described by the character will naturally bring good fortune because it makes you virtuous.

善本	shànběn	reliable text; good edition
善處	shànchù	deal discreetly with; conduct oneself well
善後	shànhòu	deal with problems arising from an accident, etc.
善良	shànliáng	good and honest; kindhearted
善心	shànxīn	mercy; benevolence
善意	shànyì	goodwill; good intentions
善於	shànyú	be good at; be adept in
善終	shànzhōng	die a natural dealth; die in one's bed

146

善罷甘休
shàn bà gān xiū
leave the matter at that; let it go at that

善破善立
shàn pò shàn lì
be good at destroying the old and establishing the new

善始善終
shàn shǐ shàn zhōng
start well and end well; do well from start to finish; see sth. through

改惡從善
gǎi è cóng shàn
give up evil and return to good; mend one's way

心懷不善
xīn huái bú shàn
harbour ill intent

善有善報，惡有惡報
shàn yǒu shàn bào, è yǒu è bào
Good will be rewarded with good, and evil with evil.

Example:

他是個很善良的人。
Tā shì ge hěn shànliáng de rén.
He's a very good fellow.

書畫叢中尋漢字

shèng

(sage; wise man)

聖

A pictogram with three components. 耳 = the ear. 口 = the mouth. 王 = the king. He who is able to listen and get the full implications of what the speaker is trying to say has the potential of being a king. That man is a sage. Compare this idea with Plato's philosopher king.

聖餐	shèngcān	Holy Communion
聖誕	shèngdàn	the birthday of Jesus Christ; Christmas
聖地	shèngdì	the Holy Land (or City); sacred place of the Chinese revolution
聖潔	shèngjié	holy and pure
聖經	shèngjīng	the Holy Bible; the Bible: Holy Writ
聖母	shèngmǔ	a female deity; goddess; the (Blessed) Virgin Mary; Madonna
聖賢	shèngxián	sages and men of virtue
聖旨	shèngzhǐ	imperial edict

神聖領土
shén shèng lǐng tǔ
sacred territory
聖誕老人
Shèngdàn Lǎorén
Santa Claus
古語云：人非聖賢，誰能無過
gǔ yǔ yún: rén fēi shèng xián, shuí néng wú guò
As the old saying goes, "Men are not saints, how can they be free from faults?"

Example:

只有聖人才能容忍她的那幾個孩子。
Zhǐyǒu shèngrén cáinéng róngrěn tā de nà jǐge háizi.
You would need to be a saint to put up with her children.

shí
(ten)

In oracle bones, a vertical line " | " denotes ten. But as numbers kept on increasing in daily life, ten became a cross, i.e., a short horizontal line has been added across the vertical line as evident in metal language " ♦ ". This enabled the numbering to go beyond ten.

十倍	shíbèi	ten times; tenfold
十成	shíchéng	100 per cent
十分	shífēn	very; fully; utterly; extremely
十足	shízú	100 per cent; out-and-out; sheer
十進制	shíjìnzhì	the decimal system
十六開	shíliùkāi	sixteenmo; 16 mo

十萬火急
shí wàn huǒ jí
posthaste; most urgent
i.e., as a mark on dispatches

十惡不赦
shí è bú shè
guilty of unpardonable evil; unpardonably wicked

十拿九穩
shí ná jiǔ wěn
90 per cent sure; practically certain; in the bag

十全十美
shí quán shí měi
be perfect in every way; be the acme of perfection; leave nothing to be desired

十字街頭
shí zì jiē tóu
crisscross street; busy city streets

Example:

這樣大的洪水真是十年九不遇。
Zhèyàng dà de hóngshuǐ zhēnshì shínián jiǔ bú yù.
A flood of this sort is really unprecedented.

shǔ

(rat; mouse)

鼠

In metal language, the rat pictogram was "🐀". Here you have "Ʊ" to represent its developed teeth, "🐁" its fast-running feet and "ʔ" its long tail. Since hoary times, the rat has always been man's enemy. It is very much hated for the trouble it causes. In Chinese, all expressions associated with the rat have derogatory connotations. For example, 鼠輩 scoundrels; 鼠竄 scamper off like a rat; 鼠目寸光 see only what is under one's nose (the eyes of a rat).

鼠輩	shǔbèi	mean creatures; scoundrels
鼠瘡	shǔchuāng	scrofula
鼠竄	shǔcuàn	scamper off like a rat; scurry away like frightened rats
鼠疫	shǔyì	the plague

Chinese Made - *Learning the Characters Through Illustrations*

鼠竄狼奔
shǔ cuàn láng bēn
run hither and thither like rats and wolves

鼠肚雞腸
shǔ dù jī cháng
suffer affronts without resentment; lacking courage or endurance

鼠目寸光
shǔ mù cùn guāng
a mouse can see only an inch; see only what is under one's nose; be shortsighted

鼠竊狗偷
shǔ qiè gǒu tōu
filch like rats and snatch like dogs

i.e., play petty tricks on the sly

Example:

我們的貓很會捕鼠。
Wǒmen de māo hěn huì bǔ shǔ.
Our cat mouses well.

shuì

(sleep; asleep)

睡

Pictophonetic character composed of 目 and 垂. On the left side is the eye symbol and on the right is a character meaning drop. When one's eyelid drops, he or she is most probably asleep.

睡覺	shuìjiào	sleep
睡蓮	shuìlián	water lily
睡帽	shuìmào	nightcap
睡夢	shuìmèng	sleep; slumber
睡眠	shuìmián	sleep
睡醒	shuìxǐng	wake up
睡意	shuìyì	sleepiness; drowsiness

睡夢狀態
shuì mèng zhuàng tài
dream state
睡眠障礙
shuì mián zhàng ài
sleep-disorder; somnipathy
早起早睡
zǎo qǐ zǎo shuì
early to bed and early to rise
睡眠不足
shuì mián bù zú
not have enough sleep

Example:

馬上上床，好好的睡一覺。
Mǎshàng shàng chuáng, hǎohǎo de shuì yí jiào.
Get straight into bed and have a good sleep.

書畫叢中尋漢字

si

(private; selfish)

私

The left side of this ideogram is the crop radical " 禾 " The right side " ㄙ " implies binding the crops into a bundle with a rope and taking it home. This conveyed the idea of ownership, something private.

私奔	sībēn	elopement
私娼	sīchāng	unlicensed prostitute
私仇	sīchóu	personal enmity (or grudge)
私憤	sīfèn	personal spite
私念	sīniàn	selfish motives (or ideas)
私事	sīshì	private (or personal) affairs
私通	sītōng	have a secret communication with

私有材產
sī yǒu cái chǎn
private property

竊竊私語
qiè qiè sī yǔ
talk in whispers

不謀私利
bù móu sī lì
seek no personal gain

私相授受
sī xiāng shòu shòu
privately give and privately accept; make an illicit transfer

私心雜念
sī xīn zá niàn
selfish ideas and personal considerations

不徇私情
bù xún sī qíng
not swayed by personal considerations

Example:

本閱覽室參考書不得私自攜出。
Běn yuèlǎnshì cānkǎoshū bù dé sīzì xié chū.
No reference books are to be taken out of the reading room without permission.

書畫叢中尋漢字

sūn

(grandson)

孫

In metal language it was "  ", the left side " 𪜁 " being the son symbol and the right side " 𢆶 " two knots tied on a string. When the two parts are linked together, this ideogram implies a continuing line of sons and therefore grandsons.

孫女	sūnnǚ	granddaughter
孫子	sūnzi	grandson
孫媳婦	sūnxífu	grandson's wife; granddaughter-in-law
子孫	zǐsūn	posterity

子子孫孫
zǐ zǐ sūn sūn
generation after generation of descendants
子孫後代
zǐ sūn hòu dài
coming generations; descendants
孝子賢孫
xiào zǐ xián sūn
worthy progeny; true son
孫子兵法
Sūnzǐ bīng fǎ
Sun Zi's Art of War

Example:

她傷心地看着她死去的孫子的照片。
Tā shāngxin de kàn zhe tā sǐ qù de sūnzi de zhàopiàn.
She looks sadly at a photo of her dead grandson.

書畫叢中尋漢字

tài
(greatest;
excessively)

太

In ancient times, 大 and 太 were the same character. A horizontal line was later added to 大 to make 太. In the oracle bones, two men were put together to make the character "𡗶", pointing to the unusual height and thus conveying the sense of greatness. In *Zhuan* language, two horizontal lines were placed under 大 to stress the greatness.

太后	tàihòu	mother of an emperor; empress dowager; queen mother
太監	tàijiān	(court) eunuch
太廟	tàimiào	the Imperial Ancestral Temple
太平	tàipíng	peace and tranquility
太陽	tàiyáng	the sun
太極拳	tàijíquán	*taijiquan*, a kind of traditional Chinese shadow boxing
太平洋	Tàipíngyáng	the Pacific (Ocean)

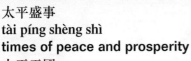

太平盛事
tài píng shèng shì
times of peace and prosperity

太平天國
Tàipíng Tiānguó
the Taiping Heavenly Kingdom (1851-1864), established by Hong Xiuquan during the Taiping Revolution, the largest of peasant uprisings in China's history

太歲頭上動土
tàisuì tóu shang dòng tǔ
provoke sb. far superior in power or strength

太公釣魚，願者上鉤
Tài Gōng diào yú, yuàn zhě shàng gōu
like the fish rising to Jiang Tai Gong's hookless and baitless line

i.e., a willing victim letting himself be caught

Example:

今天太陽很好。
Jīntiān tàiyáng hěnhǎo.
It's a lovely sunny day.

書畫叢中尋漢字

tān
(crave for;
greedy)

貪

An ideogram composed of 今 and 貝. The latter represents money or property while the top part of "𠓛" conveys the act of hiding something under the roof. 貪 therefore means hiding one's property under the roof. Later on it came to mean hankering after or greedy for wealth or other things.

貪婪	tānlán	avaricious; greedy; rapacious
貪戀	tānliàn	be reluctant to part with; hate to leave; cling to
貪圖	tāntú	seek; hanker after; covet
貪污	tānwū	corruption; graft
貪心	tānxīn	greed; avarice; rapacity
貪贓	tānzāng	take bribes; practise graft
貪嘴	tānzuǐ	greedy (for food); gluttonous

貪得無厭
tān dé wú yàn
be insatiably avaricious

貪官污吏
tān guān wū lì
corrupt officials; venal official

貪生怕死
tān shēng pà sǐ
cravenly cling to life instead of braving death; care for nothing but saving one's skin; be mortally afraid of death

貪天之功
tān tiān zhī gōng
arrogate to oneself the merits of others; claim credit for other people's achievements

貪小失大
tān xiǎo shī dà
covet a little and lose a lot; seek small gains but incur big losses

貪贓枉法
tān zāng wǎng fǎ
take bribes and bend the law; pervert justice for a bribe

Example:

她貪圖便宜在市場上買了幾條褲子。
Tā tāntú piányi zài shìchǎng shang mǎi le jǐ tiáo kùzi.
She got some trousers on the cheap down at the market.

tián

(farmland)

田

This pictogram was written like this "田" in oracle bones. It represented the ridges or ditches which separate the patches of farmland. Notice that the lines were not strictly regular, for that was what the farmland looked like in those days. By the time of metal language, the character had already become very close to its present form "⊕".

田地	tiándì	field; farmland; cropland; wretched situation; plight
田賦	tiánfù	feudal land tax
田埂	tiángěng	a low bank of earth between fields; ridge
田雞	tiánji	frog
田間	tiánjiān	field; farm
田徑	tiánjìng	track and field
田園	tiányuán	fields and gardens; countryside
田莊	tiánzhuāng	country estate

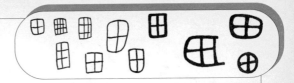

田間管理
tián jiān guǎn lǐ
field management
田徑運動
tián jìng yùn dòng
track and field sport; athletics
田園風光
tián yuán fēng guāng
rural scenery
田園生活
tián yuán shēng huó
idyllic life

Example:

你怎麼落到這步田地。
Nǐ zěnme luò dào zhèi bù tiándì.
How did you get into such a plight.

tù

(rabbit)

兔

In oracle bones, " " bears the likeness of a rabbit, emphasising its two large ears. The *Zhuan* script " " on the other hand stresses its big tail " ".

兔唇	tùchún	harelip
兔脱	tùtuō	run away like a hare; escape; flee
兔子	tùzi	hare; rabbit
家兔	jiātù	rabbit
野兔	yětù	hare
兔崽子	tùzǎizi	brat; bastard

兔死狐悲

tù sǐ hú bēi

the fox mourns the death of the hare

i.e., like grieves for like

兔死狗烹

tù sǐ gǒu pēng

the hounds are killed for food once all the hares are bagged

i.e., trusted aides are eliminated when they have outlived their usefulness

兔子不吃窩邊草

tùzi bù chī wō biān cǎo

a rabbit doesn't eat the grass near its own hole (so that it will be protected)

i.e., a villain doesn't harm his nextdoor neighbours

兔子尾巴長不了

tùzi měiba cháng bù liǎo

the tail of a rabbit can't be long

i.e., won't last long

Example:

他坐着等待一隻兔子從洞穴裡跑出來。

Tā zuòzhe děngdài yìzhī tùzi cóng dòngxuè lǐ pǎo chūlái.

He sat watching for a rabbit to come out of the burrow.

書畫叢中尋漢字

tuì
(slough off)

蛻

The left side of this character is the insect and animal symbol " 虫 ", such as 蟬 (cicada), 蛇 (snake). The right side "兑" has the meaning of sloughing off, getting rid of. This combination refers to the fact that cicadas and snakes slough off their skin.

蛻變	tuìbiàn	change qualitatively; transform; transmute
蛻化	tuìhuà	slough off; exuviate
蛻皮	tuìpí	cast off (or shed) a skin; exuviate
蛇蛻	shétuì	snake slough

感生蜕變
gǎn shēng tuì biàn
induced decay
自發蜕變
zì fā tuì biàn
spontaneous decay

Example:

我們在一塊石頭下發現了這條斑駁的蛇蜕。

Wǒmen zài yíkuài shítou xià fāxiàn le zhèi tiáo bānbó de shétuì.

We found the mottled slough under a rock.

wàn

(ten thousand)

萬

The origin of this character may be found in oracle bones, surprisingly presented as a scorpion " 𧖸 ". Now the scorpion is an awesome animal whose bites can cause extreme pain and even death. In metal language " 𧖸 ", the sign of two human hands " 𠂇 " is added to the scorpion's tail, reminding the reader that when one tries to catch a scorpion, he should first get hold of its tail. The idea is transferred to mean when a number reaches ten thousand, it becomes as terrifying as the scorpion. Notice that throughout the world, only Chinese and Indians use ten thousand (lakh in India) as a counting unit.

萬分	wànfēn	very much; extremely
萬難	wànnán	all difficulties
萬能	wànnéng	omnipotent; all-powerful; universal; all-purpose
萬事	wànshì	all things; everything
萬歲	wànsuì	long live
萬物	wànwù	all things on earth
萬象	wànxiàng	every phenomenon on earth; all manifestations of nature
萬幸	wànxìng	very lucky (or fortunate); by sheer luck

170

萬家燈火
wàn jiā dēng huǒ
a myriad twinkling lights (of a city)

萬籟俱寂
wàn lài jù jì
all is quiet; silence reigns supreme

萬馬奔騰
wàn mǎ bēn téng
ten thousand horses galloping ahead

i.e., going full steam ahead

萬事亨通
wàn shì hēng tōng
everything goes well

萬水千山
wàn shuǐ qiān shān
ten thousand crags and torrents

i.e., the trials of a long journey

萬無一失
wàn wú yì shī
no danger of anything going wrong; no risk at all; perfectly safe; surefire

萬紫千紅
wàn zǐ qiān hóng
a riot (or blaze) of colour

Example:

萬一有人找我，就請他留個條。
Wànyī yǒu rén zhǎo wǒ, jiù qǐng tā liú ge tiáo.
If by any chance somebody comes to see me, ask him to leave a message.

wěi

(submit; mild)

委

In oracle bones, it was "𦥯", the right side "𥝌" being a drooping wheat ear, and the left "𢆶" a woman sign. The combination denotes gentleness and obedience traditionally associated with women.

委派	wěipài	appoint; delegate; designate
委任	wěirèn	appoint
委實	wěishí	really; indeed
委瑣	wěisuǒ	petty; trifling; of wretched appearance
委託	wěituō	entrust; trust
委婉	wěiwǎn	mild and roundabout; tactful
委員	wěiyuán	committee member

委以重任
wěi yǐ zhòng rèn
entrust sb. with an important task

委靡不振
wěi mǐ bú zhèn
dispirited; in low spirits; dejected and apathetic

委曲求全
wěi qū qiú quán
compromise out of consideration for the general interest; stoop to compromise

委係實情
wěi xì shí qíng
actually; certainly

委過於人
wěi guò yú rén
put the blame on sb. else

Example:

對不起，委屈你了。
Duìbuqǐ, wěiqū nǐ le.
Sorry to have made you go through all this.

173

書畫叢中尋漢字

wù

(thing)

物

Originally, 物 referred to an ox with hair of mixed colours. That's why it had an ox sign " 牛 " on the left. With time, this character has come to mean thing or matter. 萬物, for example, means ten thousand things, or all things in the world.

物產	wùchǎn	porducts; produce
物價	wùjià	price
物件	wùjiàn	thing; article
物理	wùlǐ	innate laws of things; physics
物品	wùpǐn	article; goods
物色	wùsè	look for; seek out; choose
物證	wùzhèng	material evidence
物質	wùzhì	matter; substance; material

物歸原主
wù guī yuán zhǔ
return sth. to its rightful owner

物換星移
wù huàn xīng yí
change of the seasons

物極必反
wù jí bì fǎn
things turn into their opposite when they reach the extreme

物盡其用
wù jìn qí yòng
make the best use of everything; let all things serve their proper purpose

物以類聚
wù yǐ lèi jù
things of one kind come together; like attracts like; birds of a feather flock together

Example:

你已把旅行用的物件收拾好了嗎?
Nǐ yǐ bǎ lǚxíng yòng de wùjiàn shōushi hǎo le ma?
Have you packed your things for the journey?

書畫叢中尋漢字

xià

(down; under)

下

In oracle bones, this associative character looked like "⌒". The curve on top "⌒" signifies land, and the short horizontal line " ﹣ " below it indicates underneath. Notice in "‿" (up) the short line is placed on top.

下擺	xiàbǎi	the lower hem of a gown, jacket or skirt; width of such a hem
下班	xiàbān	come or go off work; knock off
下策	xiàcè	a bad plan; an unwise decision; the worst thing to do
下場	xiàchǎng	go off stage; exit
下等	xiàděng	low-grade; inferior
下賤	xiàjiàn	low; mean; degrading
下游	xiàyóu	lower reaches
下崗	xiàgǎng	be laid off

Chinese Made - *Learning the Characters Through Illustrations*

下穿交叉
xià chuān jiāo chǎ
underpass; undercrossing

正中下懷
zhèng zhòng xià huái
be exactly what one wants

下不為例
xià bù wéi lì
not to be taken as a precedent; not to be repeated

下車伊始
xià chē yī shǐ
the moment one alights from the official carriage

i.e., the moment one takes up one's official post

下里巴人
xià lǐ bā rén
Song of the Rustic Poor (a folk song of the state of Chu); popular literature or art

下筆千言，離題萬里
xià bǐ qiān yán, lí tí wàn lǐ
A thousand words from the pen in a stream, but ten thousand *li* away from the theme.
i.e., write quickly but stray from the theme

Example:

她激動得說不下去。
Tā jīdòng de shuō bú xià qù.
She was so overcome with emotion that she couldn't go on.

書畫叢中尋漢字

xiǎn

(delicious)

鮮

In oracle bones, this character is a combination of fish and sheep, either one on top of the other "🐟" or sideways "鮮". Since both fish and mutton taste delicious, the two together only serve to make the point clear to the reader.

鮮紅	xiānhóng	bright red; scarlet
鮮花	xiānhuā	fresh flowers; flowers
鮮美	xiānměi	delicious; tasty
鮮明	xiānmíng	(or colour) bright
鮮嫩	xiānnèn	fresh and tender
鮮血	xiānxuè	blood
鮮艷	xiānyàn	bright-coloured; gaily-coloured

鮮艷奪目
xiān yàn duó mù
dazzlingly beautiful; resplendent
色彩鮮明
sè cǎi xiān míng
in bright colours; bright-coloured; clear-cut; distinct
主題鮮明
zhǔ tí xiān míng
have a distinct theme
顏色鮮艷
yán sè xiān yàn
in gay colours

Example:

這塊布顏色太鮮。
Zhèi kuài bù yánsè tài xiān.
This cloth is too bright.

xiáng

(auspicious)

祥

The left side of this pictograph " 示 " means to pray or give offerings, and the right "羊" the sheep. It was hoped that by offering a sheep as sacrifice to heaven, the prayer would get an auspicious omen.

祥瑞	xiángruì	auspicious sign; propitious omen
安祥	ānxiáng	composed; serene; unruffled
慈祥	cíxiáng	kindly
吉祥	jíxiáng	lucky; auspicious; propitious

吉祥如意
jí xiáng rú yì
good fortune as one wishes
舉止安祥
jǔ zhǐ ān xiáng
behave with composure

Example:

她是一個慈祥的老人。
Tā shì yígè cíxiáng de lǎorén.
She is a kindly old lady.

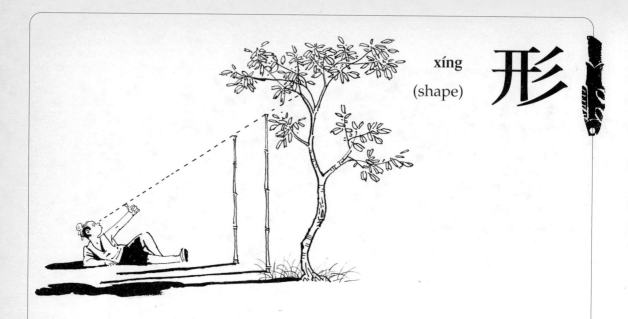

xíng
(shape)

形

To measure the length of a tree, the ancients placed two sticks " 幵 " of varying length nearby. A person lying on the ground had the tops of the sticks and the tree in a straight line and then measure the length of the shadows " 彡 " they cast on the ground. That is the reason for the use of the expression 形影 (shape and shadow).

形成	xíngchéng	take shape; form
形跡	xíngjì	a person's movements and expression
形容	xíngróng	appearance; countenance
形式	xíngshì	form; shape
形態	xíngtài	form; shape; pattern
形象	xíngxiàng	image; form; figure
形狀	xíngzhuàng	form; appearance; shape

形單影隻
xíng dān yǐng zhī
a solitary form, a single shadow

i.e., extremely lonely; solitary

形式邏輯
xíng shì luó ji
formal logic

形象思維
xíng xiàng sī wéi
thinking in (terms of) images

形形色色
xíng xíng sè sè
of every hue; of all shades; of all forms; of every description

形影不離
xíng yǐng bù lí
inseparable as body and shadow; always together

形影相吊
xíng yǐng xiāng diào
body and shadow comforting each other

i.e., extremely lonely

Example:

這個藝術團已經形成了獨特的風格。
Zhèige yìshùtuán yǐjing xíngchéng le dútè de fēnggé.
This performing art troupe has evolved a style of its own.

xiù

(smell)

臭

An associative character composed of 自 and 犬. In ancient times, the former meant nose, while the latter dog. Dogs have a very sharp nose. They can smell what other animals can't. That's why the combination means smell.

臭腺	xiùxiàn	scent gland
乳臭	rǔxiù	smells of milk (meaning immature)
臭覺	xiùjué	sense of smell
臭神經	xiùshénjīng	scent

Chinese Made - *Learning the Characters Through Illustrations*

無色無臭
wú sè wú xiù
colourless and odourless

無聲無臭
wú shēng wú xiù
noiseless and odourless

臭味相投
xiù wèi xiāng tóu
share the same rotten tastes, habits; be two of a kind

乳臭未乾
rǔ xiù wèi gān
still smell of one's mother's milk; be young and inexperienced; be wet behind the ears

Example:

純空氣是無色無臭的。
Chúnkōngqì shì wú sè wú xiù de.
Pure air is colourless and odourless.

書畫叢中尋漢字

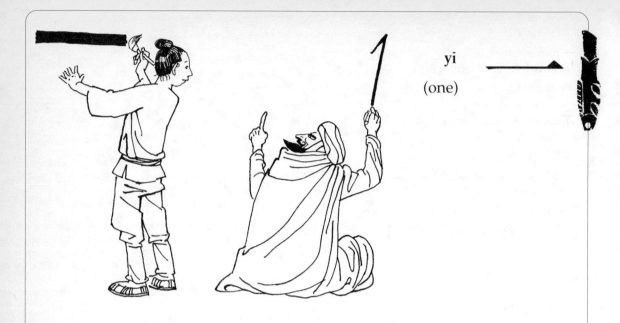

yī

(one)

The ancients used the forefinger to express the number, one. It is the smallest whole number and the first number of the decimal system. 一 in the hoary past also meant I, the pronoun for the first person singular.

一般	yībān	same as; just like
一半	yībàn	one half; half; in part
一邊	yībiān	one side
一次	yīcì	once
一道	yīdào	together; side by side; alongside
一等	yīděng	first-class; first-rate; top-grade
一貫	yīguàn	consistent; persistent; all along
一路	yīlù	all the way; throughout the journey

一塵不染
yì chén bù rǎn
not soiled by a speck of dust; spotless

一籌莫展
yì chóu mò zhǎn
can find no way out; be at one's wits' end; be at the end of one's tether

一呼百應
yì hū bǎi yìng
hundreds respond to a single call

一箭雙雕
yì jiàn shuāng diāo
shoot two hawks with one arrow; kill two birds with one stone

一刻千金
yì kè qiān jīn
every minute is precious

一脈相承
yì mài xiāng chéng
come down in one continuous line; can be traced to the same origin

一往情深
yì wǎng qíng shēn
be passionately devoted; be head over heels in love

Example:

我只跟他見過一次面。
Wǒ zhǐ gēn tā jiàn guò yícì miàn.
I've met him only once.

187

義

羊

手

戈

yì

(righteous; just)

義

The ancient form of this character "義" has a sheep sign "羊" on top and that of a hand and a dagger-axe "手" "戈" under it. This gives the idea of a forceful personality.

義憤	yìfèn	righteous indignation; moral indignation
義舉	yìjǔ	a magnanimous act undertaken for the public
義理	yìlǐ	argumentation (of a speech or essay)
義賣	yìmài	a sale of goods (usually at high prices) for charity or other worthy causes; charity bazaar
義氣	yìqì	code of brotherhood; personal loyalty
義務	yìwù	duty; obligation
義演	yìyǎn	benefit performance

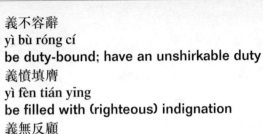

義不容辭
yì bù róng cí
be duty-bound; have an unshirkable duty
義憤填膺
yì fèn tián yīng
be filled with (righteous) indignation
義無反顧
yì wú fǎn gù
honour permits no turning back; be duty-bound not to turn back
義形於色
yì xíng yú sè
with indignation written on one's face
義正詞嚴
yì zhèng cí yán
speak sternly out of a sense of justice; speak with the force of justice

Example:

我是來盡義務的。
Wǒ shì lái jìng yìwù de.
I've come to do voluntary service.

書畫叢中尋漢字

yǐn
(drink)

飲

Originally, it looked like "飲", from which it gradually evolved to "飲". The sign on the left "會" of this ancient character represents liquor, the sign on the right "灵" is the symbol of a person with his or her mouth open in order to swallow the liquor.

飲茶	yǐnchá	drink tea
飲料	yǐnliào	drink; beverage
飲食	yǐnshí	food and drink; diet
冷飲	lěngyǐn	cold drinks
飲水器	yǐnshuǐqì	drinking bowl; drinker
飲用水	yǐnyòngshuǐ	drinking water; potable water

Chinese Made - *Learning the Characters Through Illustrations*

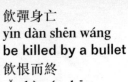

飲彈身亡
yǐn dàn shēn wáng
be killed by a bullet

飲恨而終
yǐn hèn ér zhōng
die with a grievance in one's heart

飲泣吞聲
yǐn qì tūn shēng
swallow one's tears; weep silent tears

飲水思源
yǐn shuǐ sī yuán
when you drink water, think of its source

i.e., never forget where one's happiness comes from

飲鴆止渴
yǐn zhèn zhǐ kě
drink poison to quench thirst

i.e., seek temporary relief regardless of the consequences

Example:

他賺來的錢半數花在飲酒上。
Tā zhuàn lái de qián bàn shù huā zài yǐnjiǔ shang.
He drinks half his earnings, spends it on alcoholic liquors.

右

yòu

(right)

右

From the metal language "彐" and the *Zhuan* script "彐", one can detect that the right arm is moving to pick up something. It is the movement which is presented in the character.

右邊	yòubiān	the right (or right-hand) side; the right
右舵	yòuduò	right standard rudder; right rudder
右鋒	yòufēng	right forward
右面	yòumiàn	the right (or right-hand) side
右手	yòushǒu	the right hand
右首	yòushǒu	the right-hand side; the right
右旋	yòuxuán	dextrorotation

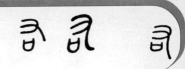

右旋物質
yòu xuán wù zhì
dextrorotatory substance

右翼分子
yòu yí fèn zǐ
right-winger; member of the Right

無出其右
wú chū qí yòu
second to none

Example:

她右首坐着一位老大娘。
Tā yòushǒu zuò zhe yíwèi lǎodàniáng.
An old woman was seated on his right.

yù
(prison)

獄

In primitive society there was no prison. When prisoners of war were taken, dogs were used to keep watch over them. That is why on both sides of this character are the dog symbols "犭, 犬". In the middle is 言 the character for speech, indicating that pows and/or criminals were expected to make confessions. Over time, 獄 has come to mean prison.

獄吏	yùlì	warder; prison officer; jailer
獄卒	yùzú	prison guard; turnkey
斷獄	duànyù	hear and pass judgment on a case
監獄	jiānyù	prison; jail
入獄	rùyù	be imprisoned
冤獄	yuānyù	an unjust charge; an unjust verdict
越獄	yuèyù	escape from prison

監獄看守
jiān yù kān shǒu
guard

投入監獄
tóu rù jiān yù
sent to prison; imprisoned

含冤入獄
hán yuān rù yù
imprisoned under a false charge

Example:

她去監獄探望丈夫。
Tā qù jiānyù tànwàng zhàngfu.
She went to the prison to visit her husband.

獄 獄 獄 獄 獄 獄

195

yuán

(beginning)

元

In both the oracle bones "丌" and in metal script "兂", a short line "●" was added to human sign "人", indicating it refers to a human's head. From this evolved the meaning of starting, beginning.

元寶	yuánbǎo	a shoe-shaped gold or silver ingot used as money in feudal China
元旦	Yuándàn	New Year's Day
元老	yuánlǎo	senior statesman; founding member (of a political organization, etc.)
元配	yuánpèi	first wife
元曲	yuánqǔ	a type of verse popular in the Yuan Dynasty (1271-1368), including *zaju* (雜劇) and *sanqu* (散曲), sometimes referring to *zaju* only
元首	yuánshǒu	head of state
元兇	yuánxiōng	prime culprit; arch-criminal

196

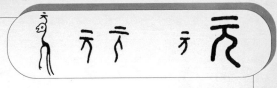

元氣旺盛
yuán qì wàng shèng
full of vitality

元素分析
yuán sù fēn xi
ultimate analysis

恢復元氣
hui fù yuán qì
regain one's strength

開國元勳
kāi guó yuán xūn
founders of a state

Example:

元旦我想請一些朋友吃飯。
Yuándàn wǒ xiǎng qǐng yìxiē péngyǒu chīfàn.
I'm going to entertain some of my friends on New Year's Day.

書畫叢中尋漢字

yuè

(music)

樂

From the oracle bones " 𝌆 " and the metal script " 𝌆 ", we could conclude that this pictograph originated from a tree-branch-shaped musical instrument. With a wooden handle " ✱ " and bells " 𝌆 " attached to it, this instrument was used during a sacrificial ceremony to ancestors. Later on it developed to mean music from the instrument. Still later it evolved to mean happiness.

樂池	yuèchí	orchestra pit
樂隊	yuèduì	orchestra; band
樂府	yuèfǔ	an official conservatory in the Han Dynasty (206 .BC.-A.D. 220) for collecting and composing folk songs and ballads
樂理	yuèlǐ	music theory
樂譜	yuèpǔ	music score
樂器	yuèqì	musical instrument
樂團	yuètuán	philharmonic society
樂章	yuèzhāng	movement

198

樂隊指揮
yuè duì zhǐ huī
conductor; bandmaster
交響樂隊
jiāo xiǎng yuè duì
symphony (or philharmonic) orchestra
古典音樂
gǔ diǎn yīn yuè
classical music
管弦樂隊
guǎn xián yuè duì
orchestra

Example:

這孩子的音樂天分確實很高。
Zhèi háizi de yīnyuè tiānfèn quèshí hěn gāo.
The kid is really highly musical.

yùn
(pregnant)

孪

In ancient Chinese, this character looked like " ". Outside " " is a human body and inside " " a foetus.

孕畜	yùnchù	pregnant domestic animal
孕妇	yùnfù	pregnant woman
孕期	yùnqī	pregnancy; gestation
孕穗	yùnsuì	booting
孕吐	yùntǔ	vomiting during pregnancy; morning sickness
孕育	yùnyù	be pregnant with

懷孕婦女
huái yùn fù nǚ
pregnant women
孕期反應
yùn qī fǎn yìng
pregnancy reaction
夫征不復，婦孕不育
fū zhēng bú fù, fù yùn bú yù
The wife cannot be pregnant with her husband away at the front.

Example:

他妻子懷孕已八個月了。
Tā qīzi huáiyùn yǐ bāge yuè le.
His wife is eight months pregnant.

zèng

(gift)

赠

The left part of this ancient pictograph "贈" is the money symbol "貝", the right side has the shape of a food steamer "曾". To add one's own money or property to the vessels of other people is therefore to present a gift.

赠答	zèngdá	present each other with gifts, poems, etc.
赠品	zèngpǐn	(complimentary) gift; giveaway
赠送	zèngsòng	give as a present; present as a gift
赠言	zèngyán	words of advice or encouragement given to a friend at parting
赠阅	zèngyuè	(of a book, periodical, etc.) given free by the publisher

贈送儀式
zèng sòng yí shì
presentation ceremony
臨別贈言
lín béi zèng yán
parting words of advice or encouragement
相互贈送
xiāng hù zèng sòng
exchange gifts
接受贈品
jiē shòu zèng pǐn
accept a gift

Example:

他把他的藏書贈送給圖書館。
Tā bǎ tā de cángshū zèngsòng gěi túshūguǎn.
He gave his books to the library.

zhě

(that; which)

者

The original version of the pictograph 煮 (to boil). We can detect from the metal script " 𤎮 " that there is a pot " ⊌ " with some food " ⼁ " inside, and the two dots " ⠠ " on top represent the rising steam. Now it has come to indicate a class of persons or things.

讀者	dúzhě	reader
作者	zuòzhě	author
編者	biānzhě	editor; compiler
長者	zhǎngzhě	elder; senior
勞動者	láodòngzhě	labour; labourer
勝利者	shènglìzhě	victor
出版者	chūbǎnzhě	publisher

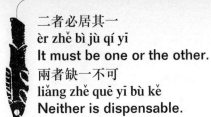

二者必居其一
èr zhě bì jù qí yī
It must be one or the other.
兩者缺一不可
liǎng zhě quē yī bù kě
Neither is dispensable.

Example:

兩個可能性中，後者比前者更可能。
Liǎnggè kěnéngxìng zhōng, hòuzhě bǐ qiánzhě gèng kěnéng.
Of the two possibilities, the latter is more likely than the former.

書畫叢中尋漢字

zhèng
(straight;
regular)

正

This pictograph originally looked like " 𝓎 " in oracle bones. The top part " ▢ " represents a city, the lower part " 𝖞 " footprints. When people walk towards cities other than their own, they are on armed expedition. That was the original meaning of this character. Now it means straight or regular.

正常	zhèngcháng	normal; regular
正當	zhèngdāng	proper; appropriate; legitimate
正好	zhènghǎo	just in time; just right; just enough
正經	zhèngjing	decent; respectable; honest
正確	zhèngquè	correct; right; proper
正視	zhèngshì	face squarely; face up to; look squarely at
正義	zhèngyì	justice

正本清源
zhèng běn qíng yuán
radically reform; thoroughly overhaul

正襟危坐
zhèng jīn wēi zuò
straighten one's clothes and sit properly; be all seriousness

正人君子
zhèng rén jūn zǐ
a man of honour

正顏厲色
zhèng yán lì sè
look serious and severe; put on a stern countenance

正中下懷
zhèng zhòng xià huái
be just what one hopes for; fit in exactly with one's wishes

Example:

現在咱們談正事。
Xiànzài zánmen tán zhèngshì.
Now let's talk business.

zhi

(lean on)

枝

支 is an associative character with two components: 十 and 又. The former represents a tree branch, the latter a hand. When a man is hard at walking, he holds a tree branch or a stick to lean on. This character 支 used to be indistinguishable from the character 枝, which now means branch or twig.

枝杈	zhīchà	branch; twig
枝接	zhījiē	scion grafting
枝節	zhījié	branches and knots (minor matters)
枝蔓	zhīmàn	branches and tendrils (complicated and confused)
枝條	zhītiáo	branch; twig
枝葉	zhīyè	branches and leaves
枝子	zhīzi	branch; twig

横生枝節
héng shēng zhī jié
raise unexpected difficulties
一枝蠟燭
yi zhī là zhú
a candle
一枝梅花
yi zhī méi huā
a spray of plum blossoms
文字枝蔓，不得要領
wén zì zhī màn, bù dé yào lǐng
The writing is confused and the main points are not clear.

Example:

那棵大樟樹枝葉茂盛。
Nà kē dà zhāngshù zhiyè màoshèng.
The big camphor tree is a mass of branches and leaves.

zì
(word; Chinese character)

字

In ancient Chinese, this character looked like "🈀". The top part "∩" is a house or room and inside "𠀉" it a child. Children are easily distracted. To make them concentrate, teachers have to keep them in a classroom to study, first of all the Chinese characters.

字典	zìdiǎn	dictionary
字畫	zìhuà	calligraphy and painting
字跡	zìjì	handwriting
字謎	zìmí	a riddle about a character or word
字母	zìmǔ	letters of an alphabet
字體	zìtǐ	form of a written or printed character
字眼	zìyǎn	wording; diction
字樣	zìyàng	model of written characters; printed or written words

Chinese Made - Learning the Characters Through Illustrations

字裡行間
zì lǐ háng jiān
between the lines

字跡工整
zì jì gōng zhěng
neat writing

字斟句酌
zì zhēn jù zhuó
choose one's words with great care; weigh every word

立字為憑
lì zì wéi píng
give a written pledge

待字閨中
dài zì guī zhōng
not betrothed yet

玩弄字眼
wán nòng zì yǎn
play with words

Example:

他寫得一手好字。
Tā xiě de yì shǒu hǎo zì.
He has good handwriting.

Index

書 畫 叢 中 尋 漢 字